MOM! I FARTED IN CHURCH

ONE TYPE A MAMA'S JOURNEY LEARNING TO
LAUGH AND LET GO

CHRISTIE CUTHBERT

CONTENTS

Edited by Taylor Henderson

Layout by Eva Moore

Cover Design by Sour Pea Design

Forward by Kelley Kitley, LCSW, Serendipitous Psychotherapy, LLC

To John, Tommy, Teddy, and Nate.
You provided the shenanigans. I simply wrote them down.
Love you to the moon and back, always.
xoxo, Momma

FOREWORD

Anxiety and Motherhood
By Kelley Kitley, LCSW

As a mom of four and practicing psychotherapist for the last 15 years, I can speak both personally and professionally that parenting can be the hardest and most rewarding job we ever have. Christie Cuthbert uses humor to lighten our load as mothers and helps us to appreciate the small moments of chaos. She owns our, often times, daunting tasks of motherhood by being brutally honest. This allows readers permission to own their own stories and a sense of relief knowing they are not alone.

One in seven women struggle with postpartum depression including anxiety, OCD, and psychosis. Many times, it's under reported and mamas are left untreated enhancing the struggle to be the best version of themselves.

Christie reached out to me a few years ago to assess her stress load and look at healthier ways to manage her anxiety. Week after week, we talked on the phone and took a hard look at some of her behaviors to make healthier choices and support her journey. In my practice, Serendipitous Psychotherapy, this is the majority of the population I treat. Women and couples ranging in age from 30-50 who are trying to manage life on life's terms while attempting to soar in their careers, relationships, finances, and parenting.

"Mom! I Farted in Church!" is relatable, hilarious, and shame free! It provides hope and normalizes some of the things we don't talk to each other about as parents. Before this book was birthed, I'd read Christie's articles published on TODAY Parents and found myself laughing aloud and saying, *me too!* I also found myself reminiscing about the toddler years of my now teenage children and wishing I had a book like this when I was starting out as a parent.

My hope is that through these pages, readers will learn to surrender and recognize they are not that powerful to manage and control all areas of life. Anxiety can be gripping and the more we learn to accept it rather than fight it, the better role models we'll be for our children and the easier we'll be on ourselves. We grow through vulnerability and parenting brings us to our knees through humility. But, when we take a deep breath and get up on our feet, we are given another opportunity again and again to learn from our experiences and do better with each situation.

It truly does take a village to raise children. Embrace all of it and don't be afraid to ask for help. It will make the ride that much sweeter and the load much lighter. Cuthbert reminds us that laughter is so good for the soul and don't take yourself too seriously. When in doubt, STOP overthinking, put one hand on your heart and one hand on your belly, and listen to your intuition.

I wish it were a life pre-requisite to engage in at least one year of therapy. We'd all be more self-aware, connected, and compassionate toward ourselves and others. Don't minimize symptoms of anxiety or depression and consult your OBGYN who can give you referrals to a therapist and/or psychiatrist. If you notice any symptoms of increased irritability, lack of motivation or disinterest in activities that you used to enjoy, difficulty sleeping or sleeping too much, poor concentration, frequent crying, feeling flat or rage, irrational thinking or behaviors, lasting longer than 2 weeks, you may want to seek help.

As a woman in recovery from substance abuse and removing alcohol completely from my life for almost 7 years, I've made it my mission to break the silence and stigma of mental health and addiction. Especially, around Mom Drinking Culture and the normalization of drinking to cope with parenting. There an easier, softer way. Don't get caught in the trap of wine culture to self-medicate, be mindful and aware of your habits. There are plenty of resources online and in person for people who have a desire to cut back or stop drinking. Moderation Management, Sober Curious groups, She Recovers- an online community of women who are all recovering from something, and Alcoholics Anonymous women's meetings have helped many women become the best version of themselves. Find something that works for you, the most important component of healing is by sharing your story and your struggles with another human being and no longer live in darkness. Find the light, be the light, and go get it girl! Namaste.

INTRODUCTION

"Mom! I Farted in Church!
Do You Think God Heard It?"

It was a warm April day in 2017 when I heard a knock at the front door. There stood my neighbor, next to my triplets, who were buck naked.

"I found these guys dancing on my lawn," he said, laughing so hard tears sprung to his eyes.

My boys' antics were a source of constant entertainment for him and his wife, who enjoyed watching the ruckus of our bedtime routine from their back porch on warm summer nights.

As I stood there staring at my boys in their birthday suits, I turned a new shade of red. My neighbor was a grandfather himself who had raised boys, so unlike me, he found the situation hilarious. Other neighbors began to gather at this point, suddenly finding themselves in the front row of the sketch comedy show that was now my front porch.

Being a Type A person by nature, I felt horribly embarrassed, like a failure. My palms were sweaty. People's false perceptions of me as "Supermom" were suddenly exposed for the chaotic truth. I needed Calgon to take me away.

I'm such a bad mom. How could my kids sneak out of the house stark naked without me even noticing? I thought. *They were down the block like dancing, R-rated lawn ornaments! They could have been kidnapped! The neighborhood must be ready to call Child Protective Services on me.*

My wild, overactive imagination immediately envisioned an anchor on the evening news reporting my downfall via teleprompter: "And in today's news, a local mom loses custody of her children after they embark on an afternoon of midday streaking. Said mom has checked into Betty Ford to cope with her existence."

That desire to appear like I have my life together has plagued me since childhood. It's something I have always battled as a Type A perfectionist. And as anyone who is Type A knows, that longing to be in control of life can't be changed—you're born with it. You can only learn to manage it, which takes time, patience, and lots of deep breathing. And most importantly, when you're sitting in the heat of the moment, it takes laughing and finding joy.

Being a true Type A person means going the extra mile to make the exterior view of your life look put-together and presentable, even when the inside is messy mayhem.

It's the reason I wake up early to shower every morning: so I can look decent at school drop-off and people won't know my head is spinning from my circus. It's also the reason I sometimes spritz my kids with body spray before school. I don't always have the energy to bathe them, and heaven forbid someone know there are nights when they go to bed with markers on their arms and sticky ice cream mustaches.

Whether it's pulling their pants down in a very public place or knocking over an entire display of seasonal air fresheners with ninja moves, my children draw attention to us wherever we go. Sometimes onlookers laugh along with us, and sometimes I get that look of pity, like I'm the old woman who lived in a shoe and had so many children she didn't know what to do.

By the way, Debra at Walmart, I saw your side-eye when my boys attempted to climb into the produce scale. Thanks for that judgment. I'm sure your kids never did anything wrong ever.

It's taken me a long time to fully embrace the idea that nothing is ever going to be perfect and that laughter is truly what brings the joy. The minute I stopped cringing and joined in on the laughs, I began to enjoy the parenting experience a whole lot more.

A year ago, my eye would've twitched as my boys hid in the milk fridge at Sam's Club. Now, I just smile and ask them to pass the half and half.

The same can be said for when they turned a visit with Chuck E. Cheese into a mosh pit and nearly knocked the mascot mouse over. They were three, and honestly, it was pretty darn funny.

And performing their "Booty Scooty" dance while at the grocery store checkout? It earns an applause, and sometimes I join in.

Being authentic with others and yourself, even when it makes you feel vulnerable, makes you more relatable and often forges friendships and a sense of community. People don't want to hear about how your child just can't get enough of the organic kale cookies you bake that taste like barf. They don't want perfection.

People want human. They want the raw, uncut realness, and they want to relate and laugh along with you.

This book is my journey from neurotic mom-to-be to a place of acceptance and joy. There is heartache, happiness, love, chaos, embarrassment, outlandish moments, and more. And every single word of it is true. As much as I strive, I am nowhere near "Supermom" status. I am just a girl, working hard to make the best of the beautiful hand God dealt me. And instead of trying to win the game, I'm having the best time I can playing along.

Throughout this book you'll learn ways to find strength, understanding, acceptance, and joy in your own motherhood experience by embracing what's truly important and letting go of what's not.

For many years, in the midst of the pandemonium that comes with raising four little boys, I had my blinders on, trying to get through each day without losing my mind. Looking back now, I can see that the challenges I faced only made me stronger. Intuition, guidance from above, and eventually learning to let go and find joy have brought me to a place of mindfulness. My hope is that anyone who picks up this book is able to find special moments in their own journey to soak it all in.

Whenever I begin to slip back into my perfectionist ways, the universe throws me a funny curve ball to remind me that finding the humorous silver linings is what it's truly all about.

The idea for this book came in the way of an extremely embarrassing moment on a Sunday morning at church. In a crowded hallway on the way into service, one of my triplets announced proudly with a huge smile, "Mom! I just farted in church! Do you think God heard it?"

A moment that would normally cause me to perspire from extreme embarrassment, instead provided clarity. God wouldn't want me to be mortified or ashamed. He would want me to laugh at the adorable little kid in front of me. He would want me to smile, not fret about what others were thinking.

"Oh, sweet Tommy, I'm sure He did," I replied. "And He's probably laughing right along with us now."

LEARNING WHO YOU ARE

A "TYPE A" GIRL IS BORN

T he dictionary defines Type A as "a pattern of behavior characterized by competitiveness, a sense of urgency, impatience, perfectionism, and assertiveness."

There are many times along your life's journey when these traits are a good thing. They create drive, confidence, and determination. The problem is, when Type A control freaks can't reach our goals no matter how hard we work to achieve them, we can feel anxious and defeated.

Throughout my extreme Type A life, I have experienced great highs and heartbreaking lows, and I'm just now beginning to find balance.

It all started when I entered the world in 1981. I gave my mom exactly 45 minutes to get to the hospital before I came barreling into the world.

I didn't even have the patience for my dad to make his way down the California coast from the San Francisco Giants game to watch my birth into this world. No, ma'am! I had things to do, like scream with colic for four months and conquer a big, wide world. I'm pretty sure if I'd been able to talk as a newborn, I would have uttered, "Bring it on, birth canal!" as I exited because I was ready to hit the ground running from day one. I was the baby of the family, and I played the role perfectly: always the center of entertainment. Never did a Christmas family gathering take place without me putting on a show with the help of my Star Stage light-up microphone set or dressing up to give a theatrical performance a la *A Chorus Line* or *CATS*. From a very early age I began creating stories in my head and would tell them to anyone who would listen.

My competitiveness as a child paired well with an

overactive imagination. I helped orchestrate a 1992 Winter Street Olympics on my block, and neighbor kids entered rollerblade ice dancing and skateboard bobsledding. We pooled our piggy bank money to buy king-sized candy bars for medal winners. With my hyper-color t-shirt perfectly coordinated with fluorescent spandex shorts and peace sign earrings, I was destined for the top honor of a Three Musketeer bar. I was convinced I was the next Katarina Witt or Oksana Baiul. And my performances were flawlessly choreographed to Kris Kross' "Jump" on mixtapes played from my neighbor's pastel boom box.

Yes, from a young age, I had a natural-born sense that if I worked hard enough at anything, I could accomplish it. That gumption at 10 meant I was convinced Elijah Wood and Macaulay Culkin would write me back from my *Big Bopper* love letters and become my crush pen pals. I was their soulmate after all, and my puff-painted t-shirt tied in a side knot and freshly permed locks would draw them like moths to a flame. They would notice the extra effort I put into my correspondence, dotting my i's with hearts and doodling amazing butterflies on the sides. I had no doubt I would be the chosen one, and when their undying affection didn't come back in letter form, I assumed my sentiments were lost in the mail. I dropped my grudge against the mailman by the time I graduated middle school. Sometimes you have to let bygones be bygones, you know?

My personal Type A drive and confidence meant

making the cheerleading team every single year and being elected to multiple student council positions. I would hound every kid on the block to work on glitter posters in my driveway well past sunset, and their payment would be Red Vines from a big Costco tub. It was a well-oiled machine, and I was determined to declare victory!

When my parents wouldn't buy me every single thing I wanted at 14, I lied about my age and got a job. When my work ethic alone wasn't enough to secure my goal, my ability to spin a story always helped me squeak by. I fine-tuned this skill in college, when I missed half a semester of media law but nailed the oral report final by concocting a lavish story in front of the class about journalism ethics. My elaboration skills also landed me on the Dean's List and in roles at community theater productions for which I was nowhere near qualified. My mom still laughs about the time in eighth grade when I auditioned for a part that required years of tap-dancing experience. I miraculously managed to fake soft shoe through the tryouts and land the role of the red-headed Harvey Girl in *Tied to the Tracks.*

In many ways, this extreme level of drive helped me create my own dreams. If you want something bad enough, you do what is necessary to make it happen, even if that's embellishing about your dance skills or on your college final essay exams.

In other ways, it made me a control freak in many facets of life. In my mind, if I worked hard enough, I could achieve and control my environment and how I was perceived. As a teenager, while my parents went through a not-so-pleasant divorce, I began fine-tuning my social media/public relations skills before the internet was even a big thing. If I looked like everything was fine and made others think all was well with my family, it was. I use this same tactic in my home now. It's always picked up and tidy just in case company happens to stop by, but heaven forbid a guest lift a couch cushion to find a swarm of forgotten Goldfish crackers—or worse, open a cabinet only to be pummeled by pots, pans, and mismatched Tupperware.

As I look back on my life, being Type A has meant many successes. After graduating college, I set off to begin my career and found an amazing Air Force Lieutenant to marry who later became a successful businessman. I saw the exact same drive in him. We are extreme opposites across the board in many ways, but our desire to kick butt, be strong, and succeed in life has always been something we understand—and love—about one another.

Being Type A also meant that I had a meticulous, time-sensitive plan in place for my life, and in my mind, all would go as planned.

How could it not?

After all, I was in charge. My goal was to be married by 24, then a new mom by 26. By 30, my writing career would be taking off, and my husband and I would welcome our third baby—a girl, who would go on to become an Irish dancing champion, big curly wig and all. Her name would be Scarlett, and she'd have red hair like her grandpa's. We'd also be in the process of buying our dream home and live happily ever after.

This was my plan, and I was sticking to it.

But God had other ideas. His journey for me to reach my dreams wasn't so cut and dry. I would still wind up with the most important, life-fulfilling pieces of my plan, but they weren't going to go on my timeline or terms.

It wasn't until I began the journey into motherhood that I realized the hard way: sometimes you truly have to throw your hands up to God and let Him take the reins.

Throughout the last nine years I've faced hardship, struggle, and chaos. I've felt pure joy, helplessness, turmoil, and inadequacy. I've experienced child anarchy, a desire to bolt out the door, snuggles so sweet they make you cry, unyielding support, and now, finally, contentment.

I spent my 20s racing to the next thing, always looking forward to what was coming next. Now I spend my 30s wanting to freeze time, having my hands full and not wanting to let go of the love inside of them.

When I began to realize I no longer had control of the big picture, my life was forever changed, shaped by the chapters that lie ahead. You too may find yourself making meticulous plans for your future self. If you learn anything from these stories moving forward, know that the only true way to get through the crazy ride and not lose your ever-lovin' mind, is to celebrate the goodness, brace yourself for the crazy, and learn to laugh along the way.

Learning Who You Are

Motherhood can conjure up insecurities, anxieties, strengths, and weaknesses we never knew existed—and often, they can be tied to our own childhood.

Take a moment to look back at your childhood. Revisit the experiences that may have shaped your personality and explore how the past directly affects the way you parent.

If some of your childhood experiences negatively impact your parenting, how can you begin to shift your thinking or actions in a way that allows you to enjoy the motherhood experience more?

2

LEARNING YOU'VE LOST CONTROL

"YOU'LL GET PREGNANT QUICKLY! ALL THE WOMEN IN OUR FAMILY DO!"

I f you're between the ages of 25 and 45, call your mother after reading this chapter and ask her how many of her friends had trouble getting pregnant.

If she's like my mom and mother-in-law, the answer will be one, maybe two. Back in their day, getting pregnant was as easy as shooting fish in a barrel, or at least that's how the stories have been retold over time. Many had the pregnancies they planned and some had occasional "oops" celebrations. Like many September babies,

I was the product of a wild New Year's Eve party that ushered in 1981. I reflect fondly on the fact that champagne and merriment were involved in the making of my being.

Now, after speaking with your mom, think about how many in your circle of friends have had some sort of trouble getting pregnant. In the 30 seconds I just racked my brain I've come up with 19 close friends, and that number would only go up from there if I stopped to think longer.

I am one of the 19 who, at 25 years young, could never have imagined the long, painful struggle I would go through for the next seven years.

"You'll have no trouble having babies," my mom would say. "None of the women in our family have. You'll have a really easy time with breastfeeding too. We were all milk cows."

Wrong, and wrong again, Mom.

My husband and I got married young, just as he was going off to fight the war in Iraq. We made the decision to enjoy being a couple for a few years before bringing kids into the picture. Our demanding, salty wiener dog and her diva-like attitude were enough to keep us busy in the early years. After Mark finished serving in the military, he attended business school at Harvard. Each time he made a move professionally, I followed along, finding a job at whichever local newspaper needed a reporter. We enjoyed two adventurous years in New England, bar hopping and taking weekend trips to New

Hampshire and Vermont to ski and admire the foliage. It was a wonderful time. But as we approached the beginning of the second year, something inside me said that it was time to grow up and start trying for a family. So, in the summer of 2007, we did just that. Being young, clinging to my mom's optimism, and once again demonstrating that Type A drive, I was confident that it would take us no time at all to see a positive pregnancy test.

But nothing happened.

Every single month, nothing happened.

Between the ovulation kits, the countless hours wasted scrolling Google and pregnancy sites, and none of it working, the control freak in me was about to lose her patience.

I began having psychosomatic symptoms because I wanted to be pregnant so badly.

"Man! I can't stop eating these M&Ms! Must be a pregnancy craving! Maybe this time it's finally happening!"

Nope. Not that time, or the time I felt tired, or the time I ate a big sandwich and was convinced my belly had grown. Not one time did I see two damn lines on the pee stick.

I swear, the amount of money I spent on ovulation kits and pregnancy tests could have bought me an entire closet of designer handbags.

It didn't help that every time I would visit home, some family friend would say, "Oh honey, you have to just stop thinking about it and then it will happen. That's how it always goes."

No, Tonya, it doesn't "always go" that way. Maybe back in the days of Tab, roller rinks, and tube socks it was that easy to get pregnant, but for my generation it's not.

And, oh, by the way, I'm Type A, so tell me how I'm supposed to stop thinking about something that consumes me from the moment I wake up to the second I lay my head down for the night?

Becoming a mother was the most important goal in my life. From the day my husband and I met, we often discussed wanting a big Irish Catholic family. For some, building an empire means erecting a huge corporation or successful career. But I knew my legacy was destined to be my family, and having no control over achieving my dream brought loads of depression and anxiety.

This was my dream, and no matter how hard I tried, I wasn't making it happen.

If I couldn't provide children, what was my role in my relationship? Would Mark want to be with someone who couldn't give him children? What would my future look like without a big, crazy family around the holiday dinner table?

I felt defeated and frustrated and had openly shared my struggles with a close friend who was about to start a family of her own. During a quick weekend trip to Chicago, my husband and I met up with my friend, and she walked in with a baby bump.

"I'm pregnant! Can you believe it?!" she said. "I'm four months along!"

I grinned, because if I didn't, I was going to start bawling. I loved her dearly and still do, and I truly was happy for her. But I was also sick with envy.

Jealous Maximus.

I wanted a bump, the ugly maternity shirts, and the excitement.

Envy is a horrible feeling. This was the only time in my life I felt it so deeply, and it made me angry. I envied every friend who announced she was pregnant while I was still having no luck. It felt as if the world was passing us by. Wanting something so badly that your longing sucks the joy out of congratulating others is a gross emotion. I believe in supporting and encouraging friends and celebrating everything. My personality is not suited for resentment.

When my husband graduated in 2008, we moved to Chicago to start our lives, and I immediately sought out one of the best fertility specialists in the city. After evaluating us both, her "diagnosis" was insanely simple and confusing simultaneously. "I can't really tell you exactly what's wrong. You look good, and you look good," she said, addressing Mark and me. "Sometimes the sperm just has a hard time meeting the egg."

Say what now?

"You're kidding me, right?" I asked. "There's no specific thing that's causing our infertility? Our organisms just can't seem to meet up? Is it like they're at a singles' nightclub and can't seem to cross paths near the bathrooms and pay phones?"

The Type A in me went on and on. This wasn't a legitimate enough answer for me.

This is medical science! It should produce a black-and-white, clear-cut answer based on data. Instead, we were left with a whole lot of gray.

Surely she is going to talk about poor egg quality or low sperm count or something I have researched the heck out of, I thought.

"So how do we fix this? Is there hope? Do I need to drink less coffee? Less wine? Up my vitamins? Seek a reiki healer? Find a surrogate? I need a plan, woman! Am I ever going to be a mom?!"

That day began my in vitro fertilization (IVF) journey that would result in miscarriages, years of pokes and prods, an ectopic pregnancy, uterine biopsies, several failed attempts, and finally, four beautiful, crazy little boys whom I told my grandma I wanted when I was 10.

How I wish I could go back and hug that girl in her 20s and tell her it would all eventually be OK. If I'm ever lucky enough to come across a genie who grants me three wishes, time travel and a crystal ball would be my top two picks.

My first round of treatment was filled with hope. Everything looked beautiful in my labs, and after the torturous two-week wait, we found out we were indeed pregnant. Our X's and Y's finally became lovebirds and shacked up in my uterus. We were overjoyed, sharing the exciting news with everyone we knew.

Eight weeks later, on a brutally cold, snowy February morning, I drove into the doctor for a 6:00 A.M. ultrasound appointment. This was my third ultrasound, and we had already seen a heartbeat, so things were looking good. I always scheduled the first appointment of the morning because I had to get back to work by 9:00 A.M., and Chicago traffic is brutal at rush hour. Coldplay's "Fix You" played on the radio as I drove into the city with my heater fully blasting. When I finally made it into the exam room that morning, the look on the nurse's face was puzzled and not reassuring. She called in the doctor, and my legs started trembling with fear of the unknown. The room was dark, and the city was beginning to wake up outside the windows. The doctor entered the room with a smile, and then I watched her face change as well. The baby's heartbeat had slowed considerably. By the week's end, it would stop completely.

Our baby, our glimmer of hope on the monitor we had prayed so hard for, was dying right before my eyes.

Many in society view a miscarriage this early in a pregnancy as "routine." After all, it is fairly common, with many women never even realizing they are pregnant before the pregnancy ends.

But for me, and anyone who has gone through fertility treatments, it wasn't an eight-week pregnancy. It was four months of early morning appointments, blood draws, injections, and drugs that make your mind go cuckoo.

And it was an entire year of hope.

I'd prayed that I'd finally get the chance to become a mom, something I'd watched several friends experience with no medical intervention at all. My sister practically winked at her husband and had a baby in her belly, I kid you not. OK, they probably did the deed as well, but it seriously happened that fast.

To say that morning was gut-wrenching is an understatement. And then to have to call each person we had told and share the awful news meant replaying it in our heads over and over again.

I felt punched in the gut. The miscarriage set off emotions in me I never knew existed. Losing hope at that level takes a while to regain. It shakes you to the core.

Dostoevsky once wrote, "To live without hope is to cease to live." In those next few days, I did cease to live. I lay on my couch, angry at God, wondering what I possibly did in life to deserve this heartache. In those moments, I felt truly hopeless.

In the weeks following the miscarriage, my husband and I would attend Sunday church service, and I would have to walk out because the minute the music started, I would begin to ugly cry. The odd thing is, 10 years later, I still haven't made it through church without tears in my eyes. I originally equated it to my utter sadness and music having a very emotional impact on my heart. Ten years later, I see it as therapeutic. It's almost as if God tells me, "I am here, and this is a safe place to let it all go."

I'm not a stereotypical church lady. I don't attend bible study, and I can't pull out any fancy, poignant bible verses at dinner parties by memory. But I do know that something within the four walls of the sanctuary moves me—a combination of release and rejuvenation. During that one hour of worship my head clears, and the beautiful sound of the music allows me to feel and face things I've pushed to the back of my mind all week. Some find that release in yoga or during a long-distance run. Mine happens in a pew while I do the ugly, fight-back-tears face.

It took another six months of appointments and treatments, and another failed attempt, before we would finally hear the good news that we were once again expecting. This time it would bring us our beautiful first-born son, John. The week we found out I was pregnant with him we moved into our dream home and I was the associate editor at our local newspaper, which I loved. My Type A plan was back on track! Yee-haw!

One would think that with this beautiful, seven-pound baby in my arms, all was calm and bright in the world and I felt at peace. But you're forgetting the Type A part of me who was already panicked that I wasn't producing enough milk, or swaddling correctly, or bathing him right. If there was a picture next to "frazzled first-time mom" in the dictionary, it would have been me, rocking a baby while feverishly thumbing through parenting books that only made my anxieties worse. I wasn't sleeping, because any tiny coo on the baby monitor would wake me from my slumber as if he were about to die. Side note to any new moms who are light sleepers: turn off the staticky, blinking baby monitor at night. As long as your house isn't the size of the Taj Mahal, you will surely hear your precious blessing from God screaming at night if they really need you. We're hardwired to hear it. Your husband, on the other hand, will likely sleep right through it. Try not to become too bitter about it. I'm pretty sure it's evolutionary.

He's not smiling at me and he's six weeks old?! I worried when reading a newborn parenting guide. *Oh Lord, I should call the pediatrician. Something is wrong, wrong, wrong!*

When I couldn't produce enough milk, I bought teas, supplements, dark beer, nipple shields, and hired lactation consultants. I developed mastitis and one night looked down and noticed the breast milk was pink because my poor tatas had suffered enough brutality and were bleeding internally. It took my husband finding me in tears trying to pump to finally agree that "enough is enough." The other women in my family may have been milk machines, but that was not my outcome despite every best effort on my part.

Motherhood is filled with these little moments of internalizing failure. In my mind, I failed at being able to naturally conceive and then I failed again at being able to naturally provide food for my baby. It made me question my worth and abilities in big ways.

"What if we lived 200 years ago?" I cried to Mark. "Our baby would die because I can't give him the food I'm made to give."

With an empathetic gaze, he smiled and said, "This is 2010, though. Let's drive to Target and buy some formula."

The feelings of failure go beyond just caring for a child. The entire experience is riddled with guilt. Some moms want to sit at home all day completely zoned in on the baby, snuggling them while listening to their little sounds. They may feel guilty for not getting out of their pajamas. Others, like me, have an inability to sit and get cabin fever. I would walk with the stroller all day long, watching the commuter trains whiz by because I couldn't handle being home. You might feel guilt for not showering all day and letting the house go to hell in a handbasket. You might experience guilt for going back to work too soon and feeling happy about it. And you might feel guilt for not wanting to sit at home and listen to coos all day. No matter what, you have mom guilt from day one in some shape or form.

Looking back now, I wish I'd been able to slow down and soak up the baby stage more, but considering the first time I was a nervous wreck and the second time there were three, I never got to truly embrace those little newborn stages.

Instead, I felt as though I was just waiting for the next cry session or the next blowout diaper.

I used to look for little opportunities to escape, like taking out the trash. My neighbors used to laugh as I was typically the only wife out plowing the sidewalks after a big snowfall. My husband would offer, but because motherhood often made me feel like a pressure cooker, I enjoyed the quiet moments in the 20-degree weather as the snow fell around me. I remember a friend of mine with twins telling me she would often stand out in the cold just for a quick break, because she became so overheated from the stress. I've done that many times. I've hidden in my garage with a bag of leftover chips from a barbecue and a glass of wine. I've posted up in my closet with my phone and a glass of Irish whiskey, wondering how I'd make it to bedtime.

We constantly beat ourselves up, but at the end of the day, the newborn phase of motherhood is really all about the mom, not the baby.

Those babies aren't going to remember a single thing in that first year of life. Those memories, photos, and the way you spend your days are completely yours to have and to hold. You want to stay in your pajamas all day and love on your little? Go for it. You want to throw your baby in a carrier and stroll the aisles at Target just for fun? That's fine too. You do you, mama!

If I could offer a single piece of advice to those bringing home their first baby, it's this: Throw away all of those how-to books and just call your mother. And if you end up like me, having to seek help to make your dreams come true, you're not a failure; you're driven to create the life you've always dreamed of.

My experience in trying to become a mother was one of my first real tastes of what it feels like to lose control of decisions in life's script. And no matter how much drive and determination you have, God works in mysterious ways. You may not always get what you want right when you want it, but it will all circle around, teaching and preparing you for things you'll face in the future.

~

Learning You've Lost Control

Nothing is more difficult than feeling a lack of control where your family is concerned. Maybe you're on a fertility journey, or maybe you have a situation with your children that's out of your hands, like illness, learning differences, or just plain old playground politics. When I struggled to conceive, my husband once said to me, "Christie, let's make one thing really clear. You will be a mom. This will happen. It may not end up happening the way you had it planned in your head, but we will have a family and you will be an amazing mother."

His words calmed my anxiety, because he was right. I could only control things I could control. I could pray, and I could do everything in my power to make it work biologically for me. If that didn't happen, then we could explore different options. What I took from his words—and what I hope

anyone struggling with a loss of control gets from this book—
is that sometimes finding control over one single thought can
open your mind to other possibilities that will eventually
make the original goal come to fruition.

I couldn't control what was happening with the sperm
and the egg, but I could do everything in my power to educate
myself, eat well, get lots of rest, and prepare my body to be a
great host.

The same can be applied to motherhood. When my day
feels overwhelming and out of control, I focus on one single
achievement for the day. The house may be a mess and the
kids may be melting down, but we all had a bath and brushed
our teeth or had a vegetable on our plate. Focusing on a few
small things you can control gives you a sense of power in the
chaotic environment that is raising littles.

3

LEARNING TO NEVER LOSE FAITH

WE CAN'T HELP YOU; CALL THE WITCH DOCTOR

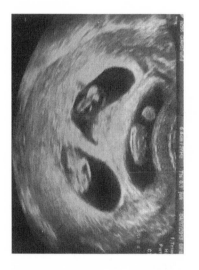

I n the summer of 2011, I was loving life. We had formed great friends in our little Chicago suburb, and I was launching a local website to help moms connect. John was 15 months old and into everything, and the idea of trying for another addition to our family was on the horizon.

One warm week in June at a neighborhood barbecue, a friend looked at me and said, "You aren't looking so good. You should go see the doctor."

That week I had been spiking fevers in the afternoons and gone to see my general practitioner, who prescribed antibiotics, thinking I had caught a little bug. But the medication wasn't helping.

The morning after the barbecue, I went to a walk-in clinic. The doctor sent me directly to the emergency room, thinking I may have contracted the West Nile Virus. I spent an entire day in the ER and even underwent a spinal tap, but no one could figure out what was wrong with me. I had a vice-gripping headache—like the worst red wine hangover you can imagine—and I began to worry as I heard doctors whisper behind the curtains about testing for meningitis and more. I had never been admitted to the hospital in my life other than when I delivered my son, so as the day progressed and I was still being held without a diagnosis, fear crept in.

The Type A in me panicked because there was nothing I could do to help the situation but lie there and wait. For six days, that's all I did: lie there in the hospital while infectious disease doctors came in to take blood and figure out what the heck was causing my body so much stress. Finally, on day six, we had an answer: I had somehow managed to pick up an acute form of cytomegalovirus, also known as CMV.

Without getting into too much medical detail, CMV is commonly found dormant in most people. Most are exposed to it as children, and it isn't necessarily harmful unless your immune system is compromised or you're pregnant. For whatever reason, I wasn't exposed until age 29, and the virus hit me like a ton of bricks. I spiked 104-degree fevers for nearly six weeks. I lost about 30 percent of my hair, was unable to get out of bed, and had horrendous brain fog. I remember one of my dearest friends stopping by with dinner and beautiful flowers, and when I went to write her a thank you note, it felt as though I had forgotten how to write. My hand and brain couldn't connect; and the words came out on the page like chicken scratch.

It was terrifying.

I had to hire full-time help for my son because I couldn't physically get out of bed. While I was fighting the illness, I felt weak and frustrated, but I still had some sense control. I knew if I kept up on medications, supplements, and rest, my health would eventually return. And sure enough, a few months later, it did.

Or so I thought.

Five months later, when my virus counts finally reached zero, I was given the green light to attempt IVF again and build our family.

I was excited, and that my pregnancy had gone so smoothly with my oldest filled me with hope and happiness about a future sibling for my son.

My excitement quickly turned to sadness and frustration yet again, as I couldn't get pregnant no matter how hard I tried. After eight more months of heartache, failed attempts, an ectopic pregnancy, and utter sadness, my IVF doctor sat me down and said, "Nothing on paper shows me why you're not getting pregnant, and I'm at the point where I suggest you see my friend who is a reproductive immunologist. She is only one of a handful in the country, and her science is still only accepted by a few, so I jokingly call her the 'Witch Doctor.'" Keep in mind this was back in 2012; reproductive immunology has since become more well-known and highly regarded.

If you're reading this book now and are either enduring fertility struggles or know someone who is, listen very carefully. A large part of getting pregnant and successfully carrying a baby to term has *nothing* to do with your reproductive organs and *a lot* to do with your immune system. A fertility specialist can pair your egg with high-quality sperm and put that little glimmer of hope inside of you, but at that point your body needs to kick in and become the St. Regis Hotel of wombs, providing the finest hospitality.

Upon meeting my "Witch Doctor," who was anything but, she explained to me that carrying a baby is a huge responsibility for the body, and if the immune system is not operating at its best, it can't and won't support a pregnancy. While my fertility doctors believed I had been ready to start trying to get pregnant again eight months earlier, my body disagreed. The Witch Doctor found I had substantial inflammation in my system from having been so sick, and over the course of four months, put me on medication and an extremely low-carb diet to normalize my system.

"If I do this, will I be able to carry another baby?" I asked.

She gave me a puzzled look and replied, "Your inflammation numbers are very high, but we'll see what we can do."

Remember that scene in *Dumb and Dumber* when Lloyd Christmas asks his crush Mary Swanson about the odds of them getting together? Mary replies, "One in a million." And Lloyd responds, "So you're telling me there's a chance!"

I was Lloyd in that doctor's office.

She didn't say "no"! She didn't say "no"! There was some small crumb of a chance I could have more children of my own, and I was about to go all out to make it happen.

Now, some people may freak out when a doctor tells them they're only allowed to eat 20 carbohydrates a day if they want success, but the Type A in me ran with it. Providing a sibling for John and growing our family, meant the world to me, and the drive and determination from yesteryears returned in full effect.

Somebody had handed me a plan. Game on! And in the meantime, I was going to go full-blown Samuel L. Jackson a la *Pulp Fiction* if one more family friend at a barbecue uttered, "When are you going to have another? This one's almost out of diapers."

Stick to grilling the hot dogs, Larry. You're better at that than probing fertility questions.

If a change in diet and medication were what it was going to take, I resolved to commit fully and follow through perfectly. And if that wasn't enough, then I would end my personal fertility journey and seek other options. I was tired of the letdowns, needles, crazy meds, and internal mind games. I was just done. This would be the final time, and I was going to give it 110 percent. There was no room for questioning whether I did everything I could. I would walk away with no regrets.

Given my circumstances, I had a 20 percent chance of getting pregnant at all—not great odds—and a 7 percent chance of getting pregnant with triplets.

Let me repeat that: a 7 percent chance.

That's about as much of a chance as a fart has in a windstorm. Six weeks later, three little farts with strong heartbeats flickered on the screen of my first ultrasound. The storm in my body had calmed, allowing them a fighting chance. In that moment, alone in the room with those blinking little images, my life would forever change...

The story of the moment I found out I was carrying triplets is an amazing tale of surprise, fear, and disbelief all rolled into one. When you go through a fertility journey, you always assume multiples are possible, and admittedly, I always dreamed about the idea of twins.

How amazing would it be to have two at once? I thought. *We would only have to go through all of the stages one time!*

In the first few weeks after my IVF transfer, the doctor's office called with my BETA number, which is basically the amount of pregnancy hormone in your blood. It showed promise.

The number has to double every 48 to 72 hours for the pregnancy to be considered viable. A high number is typically a sign of multiples. The first few calls thrilled me because, after so much heartache, I was just happy the pregnancy "took." A few weeks later, while at the White Sox opening day game with my dad, I got a call that the number had reached 30,000, which is really high.

Holy smokes! I thought. *An embryo rave party is going on inside my uterus!* I started to worry.

At 5'4", I don't have the ideal stature for carrying multiples, and my previous doctor had always told me that, should I wind up with triplets, I would be on bed rest for the entire pregnancy. With an active then-two-year-old at home still in diapers, the idea of being stuck in bed for months panicked me. It would require hiring full-time help.

On a random Tuesday, around six weeks along, I went in for a standard appointment with my Witch Doctor. My husband was at work, and I figured I'd go in, have my blood drawn, and then stop at Panera to devour a bowl of mac 'n' cheese before heading back home.

"Let's get you back into the ultrasound room," the nurse said.

"Oh, well then...this is really going down right now?"

I asked while being escorted back. Without a second to call my husband, I suddenly found myself in a dark room with my feet in stirrups. I figured we may see yoke sacs if we were lucky, but six weeks is early for heartbeats.

"OK," the nurse said in a strong Eastern European accent. "I see one...two...and three heartbeats."

"I'm sorry, what?" I replied in disbelief.

"Meesus Coothbert, you are carrying da triplets. THREE BABIES," she said, loud and slow as if I was hard of hearing.

In that moment fear washed over me. The Type A in me couldn't control the roller coaster I was stepping onto. Twins, I could handle; I have two arms. But triplets? Three babies?

"Oh my God, I don't think I can do this!" I said, my voice shaking. "My doctor told me I'm not tall enough to carry triplets!"

"Meesus Coothbert, I've had a 95-pound, five-foot-tall lady in here carrying quadruplets," the nurse quipped back. "You'll be just fine."

For some reason, the saltiness and confidence in her words gave me extreme comfort. After all, each doctor is different, and this nurse, who was working at a reproductive immunology office, had probably seen a lot of worst-case scenarios go down. The people stepping up to her stirrups are what I call "white-knuckled desperate." When you've reached the point in your dream of having a child that you're running a million blood tests and having genetic testing done, you want it bad and have pretty much hit the end of the fertility road with regard to help. If timing your ovulation, monitoring your sex positions, enduring acupuncture, meditation, and special diets, taking supplements and hormones, undergoing medical procedures, enlisting help from support groups, and praying to God and every saint imaginable hasn't worked, you wind up with this amazing, thick-skinned nurse who speaks broken English and tells it like it is.

Her sharing with me that a tiny woman who was not genetically pre-dispositioned to have tree trunk thighs and wide-set hips carried four babies, gave me a sense of confidence and drive. Yes! If that skinny little lady could do it, so could I! That sense of power began to waver as I moved into the doctor's office and waited to chat with her. My mind started swirling with all the future worries.

Three preschool tuitions, though... Shoot—three college tuitions!

Oh my God, I need a bigger car.

They want me to gain how much weight?

How on God's green earth am I supposed to potty-train three babies at once? For the love of all that's holy!

There are 30 fingers and 30 toes growing inside of me! That's beyond gross and weird!

For whatever reason the Witch Doctor's office had bad cellphone reception, so I was having a hard time reaching any of my family. The Witch Doctor advised me not to share the news with many because of the unknowns. When I finally got on the phone with my husband, I was in a total head-spinning panic. And God Bless him, he knew exactly what to say.

"We will walk through this day by day and not worry unless the doctors give us a reason to worry," he said. "You can do this, and God wouldn't have given these babies to you if you couldn't. And don't worry about the rest. We'll throw money at it, go into debt, whatever we need to do to survive. This is a blessing, and I love you."

If I could jump in a time machine, I would shoot back to 2013 and have some kind of trophy or plaque made for Husband of the Year, because mine knew exactly what I needed to hear in that moment. He knows I'm a Type A gal, and he knew just what to do to calm me: put the power back into my hands.

He was right.

There was no reason to borrow trouble, despite my difficult fertility past. The doctors said everything looked beautiful on the ultrasound and that was all I needed to ride on for that moment. I left the office that day with a 5,000-calorie, 120-grams-of-protein-per-day diet and a sense of control over my mind. Each month I'd stay in that controlled mindset by relying on a few coping strategies:

1. **Stay off the internet.** There are so many articles and horror stories out there, it's enough to put even the sanest people into a state of unbelievable anxiety.

2. **Focus on the goal.** I stuck to the rest and diet plan my doctor had given me, knowing I was doing everything I could to grow the babies and keep them well.

3. **Don't borrow troubles.** With multiples, every week they remain in your uterus growing is a good week, and there are many milestones—such as, for example, 28 weeks—when their chances of survival increase drastically. Each time we reached a milestone, we celebrated with a small piece of carrot cake. It kept our eyes on the prize and helped calm my stress about what was really going down in my body.

4. **Just keep moving.** Despite my previous doctor's recommendation of bed rest with triplets, my Witch Doctor felt the exact opposite. She wanted me on my feet, moving and continuing to work as long as I could. The blood flow and movement were good for both the babies and me. So, that's what I did.

It just so happened that the week I found out I was carrying triplets, I also found out I'd be managing a 60th anniversary gala for the organization for which I worked—and the event date was set for the week I was due. Needless to say, I worked up until the moment the babies came, then sprinted to the event with my hospital bracelet still on, making sure it went on without a hitch. Some parts of being Type A, you just can't tame.

~

Learning to Never Lose Faith

There are times in life when everyone loses faith. Maybe a relationship has come to an end or you've lost someone close to you or are faced with life-changing circumstances. It can seem easy to throw in the towel and doubt that there's a higher power guiding you. The world becomes a scary place when your faith has been compromised. You begin to feel like, Well, if this isn't going right, what else is going to happen?

Early in life I lost people very closely to me. My high school sweetheart, Steve, passed away in a car accident two weeks prior to my high-school graduation. At 17 years old, it rocked my normal and reshaped my future. The same thing happened six years later when my sister-in-law was tragically killed in a train derailment at just 22 years old. I remember being afraid to leave the house because my sense of safety and security had been ripped away.

How could God let this happen to us? How could He take such wonderful people so soon? It took a long time for my faith to be restored. Not long after my sister-in-law's passing, my fertility journey began, complete with a lot of "why me?" moments: How could all this heartache and misfortune happen to me? I'm a good person!

The answer is, simply, because life happens. My faith was

slowly restored and rejuvenated as I began to look at God differently—not as some higher power who fixes the world's wrongs, but as a guiding influence in my life. I chose to stop asking for answers and instead look for signs. Honing my intuition, trusting my gut, and living in the present have helped me continue to believe that despite all odds, good things will—and do—happen.

Time gives us so much perspective in life. When we're in the throes of stress or misfortune, which can often happen in motherhood, we begin to lose hope. But focusing solely on the day in front of us can keep our spirits up and our minds open to guidance from above. The future is unknown for us all, but today is a gift. Being grateful for the blessing of this day in front of you will build faith in the future to come.

4

LEARNING TO ASK FOR HELP

WHEN THERE ARE THREE HUMANS IN YOUR STOMACH, YOU
ASSEMBLE THE TROOPS.

W hen I carried my oldest, it was an easy pregnancy. There was no morning sickness; I easily moved around and worked up until his delivery; there were no complications to speak of; and I gained only about 30 pounds. It was an easy breezy time, and I loved every minute of people asking what I was having, giving me advice, since I was a newbie to motherhood, and the general sense of excitement around my growing belly. My son John was the first grandchild on both sides of our family, so naturally it was a "Circle of Life" a la *The Lion King* kind of moment when we announced the good news.

I had four baby showers; we sent our family on a scavenger hunt around our house on Thanksgiving to reveal his gender; and his nursery was decked out in Pottery Barn madras and rugby themes fit for a magazine spread. It was everything my Type A imagination pictured motherhood to be. I even bought a journal that matched the décor of his nursery to write to him daily when I put him down for nap.

Can we say overachiever?

Now, fast forward to three years later, when three babies were growing in my uterus, and it was a whole different ballgame. When my alarm would go off at 6:00 A.M., I would immediately go downstairs and fix a protein shake, scrambled eggs, and pour a large bowl of Cheerios—just for myself. By 8:30 A.M., after I'd dropped my son at preschool, I would hit the McDonald's drive-thru for two Egg White Delight McMuffins before heading into work and downing another protein shake, two hardboiled eggs, and a Greek yogurt, all before 10:00 A.M.

Baking three babies is no joke, and the amount of food required to ensure they grew big and strong early in the pregnancy was like competitive eating on steroids. Knowing that multiples can come early and unexpectedly, doctors want you to beef up those babies as much as possible early on, so you basically eat your face off to a level of disgust every single day.

I can remember nights spent at the kitchen table with me devouring two extra bowls of cereal at 10:00 P.M. and my husband glancing over with an "are you serious?" look on his face.

"I'm growing three lives over here!" I would yell back. "Look away!"

Doctors expected me to put on 75 to 90 pounds, and by the end of the pregnancy my face and body were so swollen that some friends didn't even recognize me during a Target run. It was actually more like a Target waddle, considering I could barely move and cruised the Dollar Spot in a motorized cart.

One day, wearing stretched-out yoga pants and an old, bright blue Harvard t-shirt of my husband's, I plopped into the car with a hankering for a Wendy's Frosty. I felt like Violet Beauregarde from *Willy Wonka and the Chocolate Factory*—round and blue—but I didn't care.

Mama needed a Frosty!

The Wendy's employee handed me my drink through the drive-thru window and uttered, "Oh, heavens! There has *got* to be more than one baby in there!"

Mind you, I was sitting in my car with a seatbelt on. She didn't even witness the full, 180-degree catwalk turn and still knew instantly that I was packin' multiple chirruns up in my uterus.

Unlike my beautifully curated registries of 2010 and four lavish baby showers, with triplets, things got real. A group of wonderful friends threw me a "Pampers and Pinot" shower, where everyone came with wine and diapers because, let's face it: that's what you really need when faced with bringing home a crowd of infants. I was also blessed to have other friends with multiples who loaned me all their gear, and between their car seats, rockers, and my own stash from the first time around, I had plenty of contraptions to care for my new babes. Those with little girls even loaned me baby dolls, so I could prepare John, then three years old, for what was about to rock his world. Each time a baby would come home from the hospital, I would take one of the baby dolls away until he had his three brothers. Trying to explain to a toddler that mommy has three babies growing in her tummy and his world is about to be flipped upside down, is not easy, and it confused and stressed him out beyond belief. But the moment he finally met them, it all clicked, and he has been the most amazing big brother ever since.

Unless they touch his stuff. Then it's all-out war.

Toward the end of the pregnancy, I started to realize why having a longer torso and being taller in stature is important for carrying many babies. Two of my boys, Babies A and B, chose their seats side by side at the bottom of my tummy, while the third, Baby C, chose the penthouse, up high near my ribcage. At only 5'4", I didn't offer much space in my cramped quarters, so every movement stopped me in my tracks. A and B, later known as Tommy and Teddy, constantly fought for room, which felt like WWE wrestlers rumbling on top of my bladder. Meanwhile, Baby C, my Nate, was chillin' like a villain pressed up against my lungs. It was like having a possessed alien inside my body and my full-time job was to work hard to keep it in longer.

While I hadn't suffered ill pregnancy side effects with my firstborn, I had every single one amplified with my triplets. Heartburn, reflux, horrendously swollen feet and ankles, backaches, hemorrhoids, peeing myself—you name it. Many nights toward the very end, I wound up in tears from the sheer discomfort of it all. But I knew I needed to hang on.

On September 30 of 2013, I was at work, finalizing things for the upcoming gala I was managing, when I started to feel like I was having menstrual cramps. My boss told me to call my doctor and get checked out just in case, so I went to the hospital. I was 31 weeks at the time, and with triplets, 32 is considered full-term.

"You're having little contractions, Mrs. Cuthbert, and we're going to keep you here until the babies are born," the doctor said.

When they would arrive, we didn't know, but I wouldn't be leaving the hospital until they were here, which was a crazy thought.

The Type A in me had done everything I could to prepare for this moment. We'd arranged for someone at work to help throw the gala, a month prior we'd hired the most wonderful nanny on earth, and we were working on a night nurse to help after we returned home.

My mom flew in to help, and after a few days in the hospital, on medication to stop the contractions, the doctor announced that I'd hit the 32-week mark and that she was going to take me off of my medication and let the babies come.

"OK, awesome. So we're going to go back for a C-section now, right?" I asked, my eyes hopeful and full of joy, fully expecting to get these kiddos out ASAP and relishing in the idea of taking my first full breath in eight months.

"No, ma'am," she said. "We're going to let them come on their own time. Every minute they are in there cooking is a good thing. We're waiting until you actually go into labor."

If you were to ask my husband about this very moment, he would tell you he has never seen an uglier cry in his life. The Type A in me thought this was a done deal. I had made it to 32 weeks! That was the goal set forth! Now, get these precious little cherubs out of my body!

Nope, that wasn't going to happen.

God was going to bring those babies into the world on His time. So, for the next few days, I continued to watch garbage TV and go for rides to the hospital cafeteria in a wheelchair while snacking on PB&J sandwiches and root beer.

Finally, on the night of October 9th, after having take-out for dinner with Mark, he went home to get our son to bed, and my mom stayed back with me to watch *Dancing with the Stars*. She could tell something wasn't quite right.

I had a lot of pressure in my stomach, although they couldn't find any contractions happening on the monitors. I eventually wound up on all fours on the bed, unable to get comfortable. The doctor rushed in to check me and announced to my mom, "These babies are coming, and they're coming fast. I'm going to go call all my people. You go call all of yours."

Within seconds, nurses whisked me off to the operating room, and my mom frantically called Mark, who had just sat down at home and poured a well-deserved end-of-the-day cocktail. As the anesthesiologist propped me up to insert my epidural, I repeatedly apologized to my awesome nurse, Karen, as I was convinced I was peeing on her at that very moment.

Having triplets required an operating room filled to the brim with doctors and nurses. There was a team responsible for me and then a team for each baby. Neonatologists, respiratory specialists, pediatricians, and more filled the room as I lay there shouting, "Where the heck is my husband?!"

Thankfully, we lived about a mile from the hospital, so he returned to the hospital just in time for them to begin the caesarian section. I'd known all along that the birth would be a C-section, but still, I was particularly freaked out about being cut open while awake. I'd ended up having a C-section with my oldest after 18 hours of labor that didn't progress, but I'd been put under anesthesia for the procedure because when they went to cut, I could feel it. So needless to say, I was kind of paranoid about scalpels anywhere near my tummy.

In that moment, when you're about to deliver three preemie babies, all you care about is one thing: hearing their little cries. At around four pounds each, the babies were too small for chest time and would be immediately rushed off to the Neonatal Intensive Care Unit after birth, so I had to rely on my husband to report on the events from the other side of the curtain to know everyone was coming out all right. There are no pictures of the triplets' birth because he was busy cutting three umbilical cords, and the few he did capture were on a phone he later flushed down the toilet by accident. I don't remember much of the next few hours—I think I was wheeled off somewhere near the OR to recover. Then at about 2:00 A.M., I was finally wheeled back to the NICU to see my baby boys.

Exhausted and still hopped up on pain meds, I lay in the hospital bed with tears of joy rolling down my cheeks.

They were here.
They were alive.
I had done it.

I'd accomplished the hardest thing I had ever attempted in my entire life, and yet the road was just beginning in so many ways. I had never been prouder of myself. My heart truly felt as if it might burst with joy. Other than a few nurses off in the distance, Mark and I were alone in the NICU with the boys. As I lay there looking at their little hats with their names on them, I felt this overwhelming spiritual presence, almost like relatives who had passed were there witnessing these little miracles with us.

Being only a few hours old, the triplets had tubes taped everywhere. Monitors surrounded them, beeping and lighting up constantly. Tiny homemade signs displaying their names with blue polka dot ribbon were attached to their isolettes.

By 3:30 A.M., I was finally wheeled to my room, also known as the princess suite. At this particular hospital, those having multiples were sent to the Four Seasons of rooms, complete with a separate sitting area with a flat-screen television for the caravans of family and friends who would surely visit.

I took a deep breath for the first time in eight months and closed my eyes, feeling all was right in the world.

Thirty minutes later, someone woke me up to take vitals, because let's face it, ladies: you don't get to sleep while in the hospital. People constantly check you—and I mean constantly. They want you to pee, get up and walk, have your blood pressure checked, loan them the tabloids you brought with you to pass time (true story). It's actually great practice for later, when you once again attempt to sleep while children saunter in your room, poking your head and telling you they're hungry or they've peed themselves.

Once I was released from the hospital a few days later, the babies stayed for a few more weeks, to grow and learn to eat and breathe correctly on their own. Each day, I would get my oldest son off to preschool and then head to the NICU, where I'd rock the babies or help them learn to feed. My husband and I would head back after putting John to bed, to rock them to sleep, sing lullabies, or just watch their miniature faces make silly smirks and grunts while they passed gas. For preemies to be released from the hospital, they must go 24 hours without a Bradycardia episode. That's when the baby's heartrate drops quickly and continues erratically. When you sit in a NICU, you can't help but stare at your baby's monitors, and when they have a "Brady" episode, a loud beeping alarm signals the nurses. Even though the nurses always have things under control, as a mom you can't help but panic every time it goes off.

Because having tiny preemie triplets in the NICU produced a lot of anxiety, I felt much relief knowing they were so close by. Many friends recommended I give birth in downtown Chicago because of the amazing hospitals. But I chose to stay in my suburban community, and during those three weeks of NICU commutes, it reassured me to know my babies were just a half-mile down the road.

In many ways, I was relieved for the babies to spend a few weeks in the NICU, where highly qualified people could care of them. It gave me some time to sleep and physically recover so I could be at my best for my oldest and the triplets' impending arrival home.

During the three weeks of limbo, I had many moments of clarity where I realized, *Oh man, the babies really are going to come home at some point. How the heck is this going to go down?*

Soon, three tiny living beings, who wouldn't sleep through the night for at least seven months, would all be under my care. These little people would need to be fed, changed, and bathed. Good Lord above, would I ever have a moment to myself again? Would Mark and I ever travel again? Enjoy a date night? Would I ever leave my house? How was I ever supposed to shower with three babies loose in my domicile? Would my house forever look like a display at a baby store, with play mats, Jumperoos, and Exersaucers replacing my velvet sitting room chairs and Pottery Barn throw pillows?

The Type A in me came out in full force. I set feeding routines, coordinated outfits, and concocted sleep schedules. If I was going to manage it all, it would require all of my Type A skills, like being super organized, to make it all happen. What would carry on in the next year of our lives would rival Golden Globe Awards nominees for Best Drama, Best Musical, and Best Comedy. God once again reminded me that life happens the way it wants to, without any bullet-pointed timelines or projection graphs. And when the going gets messy or absurd, all you can do is laugh.

Faced with being completely outnumbered, Mark and I knew we needed to hire help fast. But trying to find someone who wants to watch triplet newborns and a toddler is not an easy task. And if we did find someone who was up to the workload challenge, would they be the right fit for our family? Asking someone to spend 40 hours a week in your home with your children is an intimate decision, requiring many levels of compatibility. It involves much more than hiring someone for a regular job.

I started searching via agencies and nationally acclaimed web services, and then one afternoon I received a mass email from a friend of a friend who was moving away and looking for a new family to employ her current nanny.

I immediately replied and set up a date to meet this woman, who had handled twins and an older sibling. Knowing I was probably her tenth interview—and that the other families likely included one or two kids, not half of a basketball team—I was nervous and quasi-desperate leading into our meeting. I had never officially paid someone to help in my home, so the entire situation felt strange to me. And knowing this person would play a huge role in my children's discipline, nutrition, character development, and more for years made the decision even more important.

Part of me felt desperate to get help in the door, and part of me felt nervous about finding the right fit, a person who would raise my kids the same way I would.

This person would be in our home 40 hours a week and see the good, bad, and ugly, so it was important that our personalities meshed.

Prior to meeting Kari, I'd interviewed two others who left me feeling "meh."

Kari bounced in my door on a sunny summer afternoon, sporting a fluorescent-colored yoga outfit and fun bicep tattoos to match. She was a bright-spirited yoga instructor and nanny who had emigrated from Bulgaria as a child. She preferred working with boys (score!) and had a no-nonsense approach to bad behavior paired with a kind heart and twinkling eyes (score again!). She spoke 100 miles a minute, and within minutes, I just knew.

She agreed to come aboard the crazy train and began working with my oldest son while I was close to giving birth. The day she came to the hospital to visit the babies for the first time was magical. She had this look of wonder in her eyes, knowing that she was going to spend the next several years of her life with these tiny people. She cried; I cried; and for the next almost four years, we united as a team, achieving the impossible feat of successfully raising four boys under the age of four.

While Kari helped during the daytime hours, a Jamaican night nurse named Kharel assisted with nighttime duties the first three blurry months. She was beautiful, spoke very fast with an accent, loved my babies fiercely, and took a no-nonsense approach. Before she left at 8:00 A.M. each morning, she made sure to give my big three-year-old a huge hug and remind him how important he was, which I cherished.

The babies still lived in the NICU when Kharel and I met, and I worried constantly about whether I would be enough—not only for them, but also for John. I imagined my big boy wanting to read a book or snuggle and being unable to give him what he'd once had because I would be busy managing three infants. Worry over the first child is universal for moms preparing to have a second baby.

The day Kharel came to interview with us, she said something I will never forget and that I often share with other expectant moms who already have a little one at home. Kharel said, "When these little babies come home, keep John the focus of your affection and attention. When babies are infants, they need to eat, be changed, and be swaddled, but they are clueless as to what's going on around them. That precious little boy over there is very aware of his surroundings. Love him and make him feel special."

She was right, and it was the best advice imaginable because our now nine-year-old is the most well-balanced sibling of multiples I know. Since he was three, he's had to watch people go nuts over his triplet brothers, sometimes almost acting as if he doesn't exist. We've always gone above and beyond to point out "their amazing big brother" when chatting with people in public. And he's always had special one-on-one time with Mom and Dad and known he holds a unique role in our family.

At the time of the triplets' arrival, our home included a large bonus room down a hallway within the master bedroom. It was probably meant to be turned into lavish closet space or a private office, but we made it into a nursery. During the nights Kharel was with us, my husband and I would sleep in the guest room and give her the master suite to take care of the babies and have her space. Every night that she arrived at 10:00 P.M., it was as though a saucy Jamaican version of Mary Poppins entered our house. She would find Mark and me staring at the clock while the babies rocked in their swings. During those first few months, which we lovingly refer to as the Dark Ages, we had three fussy, ticking time bombs. We were always on edge, waiting for one of them to lose their mind.

Kharel would immediately swoop up the babies and bathe them in the sink while singing to them. Once they were clean and swaddled, she'd give them bottles and get them down for bed. My boys weren't sleeping through the night by the time she left us three months later, but they were on a regimented, unified sleep schedule. If one woke up to eat, they *all* ate and then proceeded to go back to sleep together. Kharel's magical work in making this happen soothed my Type A soul because it provided structure. When bringing my little guys home, I worried how the nights would go. The idea of never sleeping again terrified me. Like any mom with four kids, I still get nowhere near the needed amount each night, but Kharel set forth a plan of action that helped us to survive the entire first year.

Night nurses are crazy expensive and difficult to find. At least in the Chicago suburbs at the time, it was an underground, "I know a guy" situation to catch a lead on a potential hire. And when bringing home three preemies, you want the best. In the weeks leading up to their birth, I did my best elbow-rubbing and engaged in some heavy interest-dropping conversations to try to strike up leads. My attempts weren't fruitful, but others informed me that the best place to find someone was in the NICU.

"Ask around while you're there rocking the babies," a labor and delivery nurse said. "Oftentimes the nurses there know someone who is night nursing on the side to bring in some extra money."

A baby-watching side hustle!

I was intrigued—and about to attempt my greatest smooth-move sales pitches of the decade.

My mom and I immediately became those 15-year-old kids in front of the liquor store trying to find someone to buy them wine coolers. We'd rock babies and strike up leading conversations with the staff that went a bit like this: "So, *ahhhhh*, this is going to be quite challenging when all three are home! If only there were some amazing, qualified nurses who were interested in helping us with them for really good pay... Like, we'd pay *really* well. Cash money. Anyone here like Benjamins? Dolla dolla bills, y'all?"

Ears perked up.

We quickly learned in the night nurse subculture that you pay to play, and the cost of overnights with triplets was enough to put one of our children through college. But when I look back at that time, it was the greatest money ever spent.

Most babies are particularly fussy by nature between six and 12 weeks, and one of our triplets had colic. What most parents know as "the witching hour" sounded more like a satanic ritual being performed in our home. A friend gave us an inside tip that babies love the sound of oven fans, so during the evening hours, when our home morphed into a scene from *The Exorcist*, we'd "cook the babies," meaning put them in their car seats on the stovetop while the fan ran on full blast. The one with colic also got a mesh headband around his pacifier to hold it in. You've gotta do what you've gotta do to survive, people.

Having Kharel as part of our team was so crucial for our sanity in those early months. For 10 blissful hours, four nights a week, we slept peacefully, knowing someone highly qualified was taking care of our babes— even if we could've afforded a new car on her salary.

If you have the means, dig into your savings to protect your sanity. It will be worth it, I promise. I don't consider the money to be spent on sleep. I consider it a financial contribution to our mental health.

A good friend who had twins and no night help once told me she remembers being so sleep deprived she thought she saw things climbing up her walls. That's the chapter they don't include in *When Expecting Multiples*: how you will lose your sanity and be willing to sell a kidney for a solid night's rest.

⌣

Learning to Ask for Help

It's often said that twin moms are crazier than triplet or quadruplet moms. Because they have two arms and two babies, twin moms feel like they're capable of doing it all on their own. When you have three or four, you know from the starting gate you can't handle it all and need to ask for help.

We all know the saying "it takes a village to raise a child," but often, moms don't ask for help. We may be stubborn or afraid of judgement. Maybe we're afraid our need for help will be seen as weakness or failure. Or maybe we're particular about how we want things done and are worried others won't love our children enough or care for them on the same level we would.

Having multiples forced me to ask for help—something I wasn't very comfortable doing but that essentially saved my life. Whether you are just starting out your motherhood journey or deep in the trenches, know that admitting you need help can be freeing. Allowing trusted people to come in and help with your kiddos, can give you the breaks you need to be a better mom and enrich the lives of your children. Because I chose to reach out and hire help, my boys have a special bond with Kari that will last a lifetime. We still visit, and now they get to dote on her new baby boy. While asking for help from others may feel like you're losing a little control, focus on the possibilities and forged relationships it may bring.

5

LEARNING NOT TO WASTE PRECIOUS TIME

NOBODY HAS TIME FOR THAT.

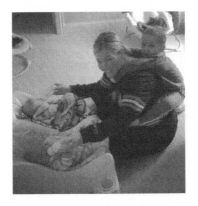

W hile we prepped for the arrival of the triplets, my small community at the time rallied on our behalf, and each day I came home to baby gear, clothing, and more on our front porch. One large box contained hundreds of bibs, which, as any mom knows, new babies go through like toilet paper. Every 30 seconds for the first year of their lives, someone was spewing all over the place. Cleaning up baby puke kept me busier than a one-legged cat trying to cover its poo.

One time, a triplet, who will remain nameless, spit up into my mouth while I was lying on the floor holding him up in the air like a jet plane. It still goes down as one of the grossest parenting moments of my life, and it still trumps my husband getting toddler poop lathered into his hair while watching the Super Bowl. We're still debating whether said child will be written out of our will.

Needless to say, you can't have enough bibs and washcloths with three infants, so we had bins all over the house filled with random hand-me-downs.

One night when the babies were about five weeks old, I was dying for a night out. A friend in town was having a small holiday get-together with fellow moms, so I talked my husband into staying solo with the boys for two hours so I could breathe a little. I had put my oldest to bed, and all of the babies were fed, swaddled, and in their rockers. All Mark had to do was watch TV, feed them again, and change them an hour later. In the early months, Tommy and Teddy looked a lot alike. Nate, however, had a red birthmark on his forehead, so he was easy to detect. Mark had a difficult time deciphering the other two except during diaper changes. Tommy had bad colic and, as a result, terrible diaper rash for the first few months. Therefore, my husband lovingly referred to Tommy and Teddy as "Butts" and "No Butts" Cuthbert.

As I returned home around 9:00 P.M., feeling tipsy and rejuvenated from the adult conversation, Mark appeared worse for the wear.

"What's wrong? What happened?" I asked.

"What the what is this?" he said, holding up a bib that had a ribbon tie as the fastener. "Seriously, you have to tie this bib around the baby's neck and into a bow! A FLIPPIN' BOW, CHRISTIE! Ain't nobody got time for this."

I couldn't stop laughing. He was completely unhinged. It wasn't the babies that were driving him nuts, but the lack of efficiency in the garment protection attire.

"What kind of Satan-worshipping person gave this to us?" he continued, giving me the death stare and walking the bib over to the trash. "Never again! Bye, bib. Bye!"

The bib probably belonged to some kind soul who likely wasn't rushed to feed three at once. It was quite pretty to look at and probably had been purchased at an upscale boutique. But when you've got an army of infants all wanting food at the same moment and screaming their heads off until they get it, ain't nobody got time for ribbon ties.

You also ain't got no time for snaps. Baby pajamas containing snaps of any kind must be manufactured in hell—that's the only explanation for them. Why, oh, why are we still dealing with snaps to secure clothing in 2019 when we have wonderful, time-respecting tools like zippers and Velcro? Do people enjoy the finger cramps that ensue after attempting to hear that little *pop* while securing a onesie? I certainly don't. Snap pajamas multiplied by three babies will probably mean early onset arthritis for me. I despise snaps. Get with the times, baby corporations! The future is now!

Over the last five years, I've picked up quite a few parenting hacks that can help fellow mamas deep in the trenches and those preparing for battle. Whether you have multiples or just one baby, time is time and sanity is sanity. So, here's a list of ways to simplify your life so you can learn to laugh and let go a bit at the same time:

- **Invest in a bottle-propping pillow.** Right when we brought home the triplets, someone told us about these special pillows you can order on ebay that will perfectly hold up a baby's bottle while they eat. Having three babies who would not hold their own bottles until past four months old, we had no choice; we had to give these pillows a try. People, these were the biggest lifesavers we've ever owned. The pillow itself looks like a stuffed bib covered in soft fabric with a scrunchie sewn on the top of it. You simply place the pillow on the child like a bib, and slip the bottle through the scrunchie and into the baby's mouth. The babies loved them and batted the pillow away when they were done. Had we not invested in these I wouldn't have even been able to pee because my entire life would've been consumed with feeding people.

- **Skip the baby pedicures.** When my oldest was four weeks old I cut him while trying to trim his baby nails. I have never once clipped any since. Our nanny did trim the triplets' nails when they were babies, but now the four of them have basically turned into monkeys, biting their fingernails and toenails to the length they desire. Trimming 40 fingernails and 40 toenails would take me an entire day. Ain't nobody got time for that.

- **Double-bag your crib sheets.** This was another impressive hack our night nurse passed along. When we discussed what supplies she'd like for nighttime, she asked me to buy extra crib sheets for all three mattresses. I quickly saw why. She'd make the boys' cribs by putting on one crib sheet, then the waterproof mattress cover, and then another crib sheet on top of that. This way, if something happens in the middle of the night, like a diaper leak or spit up, you can quickly pull off the top sheet set and get the baby back to sleep quickly without waking them too much. I still use this tactic for when my boys have the occasional accident overnight.

- **Omit shoes with laces of any kind.** Honestly, unless they can tie them themselves, it's a no for me, dawg.
- **Donate to read-a-thons and other fundraisers without participating.** If you're in a financial position where you can make a small donation instead of participating in the whole online read-a-thon, walk-a-thon, whatever-a-thon in preschool and elementary, I highly recommend it. This is probably more of a nuisance for moms of multiples than most others, as each time the triplets' school holds one of these fundraisers, I have to log on and create a separate account for each child. The triplets drive me crazy with requests to set up their accounts because registering means they get a prize at school that consists of a one-cent bouncy ball or plastic ring. As if setting up the accounts isn't enough of a time suck, then the software urges me to share donation requests via email and every social media platform I possess. I love my family and friends too much to hit them up several times a year—times three— so I simply explain to their teachers at the beginning of the year that I will make a donation. Because ain't nobody got time for that.
- **Use a paper wristband when visiting public**

places. Each year my husband and I throw a massive St. Patrick's Day party, and one time we had to order wristbands for entry. With hundreds of extra neon green bands sitting in my house, I began using them to tag my kids when we went out in public. Whether we visited the zoo or the mall, I wrote my name and phone number on my boys' wristbands in case one (or more) skirted off. I also always try to dress my boys the same and in bright colors when I know we're going somewhere busy, such as an amusement park. It helps to spot them easily in a crowd. Ain't nobody got time to lose a child.

- **Consider a crib tent.** These saved my life. Had it not been for crib tents, my boys would have been busting out of their rooms the minute they could climb. Removing them instantly numbered our crib days, as the boys would climb out and get into shenanigans during nap time. The final straw was when one triplet got a hold of a large, ceramic piggy bank and decided to break it over another one's head while he slept. That was the day their nursery became a padded cell with nothing but blankets and mattresses on the floor. Ain't nobody got time for babies on the loose.

~

Learning Not to Waste Precious Time

There's something about becoming a mom and having a little at home that amplifies your impatience with the world around you. A long red light at an intersection while a toddler melts down in the back seat—or better yet, someone writing a check in front of you at the grocery store while your kids climb out of the cart—is maddening!

Assessing your mom life and where you spend your time and energy can do wonders for your anxiety. When you manage your time more efficiently, we're altogether happier people. Finding ways to simplify or eliminate time sucks allows you more time to enjoy the experience and be present. Have those groceries delivered. Skip out of that meeting you don't really need to attend. Toss muffins at the kids for breakfast in the car while racing to school. Cut out the nonsense and focus on what's important: raising good little humans and being happy.

6

LEARNING TO LAUGH THROUGH THE FURY

HOW TO RAISE LIARS, THIEVES, AND BULLDOZERS

I remember my mom having a conversation with my brother and me when we were home one summer on college break. Our town had just named her "Educator of the Year," and she was pleading with us to maintain good reputations and not wind up in the police beat section of the newspaper for our vacation shenanigans.

This is a nice place to interject the obvious side note about my mom: she, too, suffers from being Type A, hence her wanting our family to maintain good standings and appearances in our small little California town. Having your name run in the police beat when you live in a tiny community is like being on the front page of the *National Enquirer*. Grannies are most definitely going to talk, and your friends' parents will most certainly deem you a bad influence. Even now, after recently attending my 20-year high school reunion, my friends and I can still recall the names of those who made the blotter.

By the skin of my teeth, I never made it into the actual police beat, but I did cause a cheerleading squad scandal when I threw a huge party at my house after a game and a fight broke out. It's not so great when the cops show up and cheerleaders still in their uniforms are fleeing the scene—let that be a lesson to the young folks. A vice principal also accused me of cheering at a basketball game while high on drugs, even though it was really just a bad case of pink eye coming on from sharing mascara with a friend. My point in divulging my high school shenanigans is that teenagers test the waters and learn boundaries. And guess what? Many who were thought to be trouble actually grew up to be upstanding members of society and do things like write books. We all just need to be patient with that developing frontal lobe, people.

One night when I was 15 and had my learner's permit, my friend Lisa and I were sitting around the house, bored out of our minds. My mom and sister had gone to dinner and shop at a mall about 45 minutes away, so we figured we had a decent block of free time.

Suddenly, the thought struck me. "Let's go to the movies!" I proudly suggested.

While I didn't have an actual license yet, I had spent countless hours in the Costco parking lot learning to drive a stick shift on a 1989 Volkswagen Jetta and thought, *What the hell? I can get us to the movies and back.*

Keep in mind this was 1997, so there weren't any cellphones to call and check on my mom's location. Our teenage brains thought this was a terrific idea, and off we went, like Thelma and Louise out on our own adventure. What could possibly go wrong, right?

Should I get pulled over, I had my sister's I.D. to get me by. My impulsive, driven teenage brain paid no mind to the fact that I could potentially be charged with driving without a license, identity theft, and false impersonation. Again, guys, that frontal lobe was still figuring things out. My confidence radiated, and Lisa and I set out to the next town over to watch *My Best Friend's Wedding.*

A few miles in, we noticed a car turn around and begin to follow us. Convinced it was a police officer clocking our speed, we began to panic. My palms sweat as I clenched the steering wheel and prayed the car would turn. But it didn't, and as it got closer, riding my tail, we recognized the car.

It wasn't the police.

It was my mom's Volvo.

I could see the steely glare in her eyes in my rearview mirror. By happenstance, she and my sister had cut their shopping trip short and witnessed us cruising down Santa Theresa Boulevard.

"Lisa, it's my mom!" I screeched. "What do I do? What do I do?"

After a brief moment of panic, she looked straight at me and said, "Just keep going!" Because to us at 15, that made the most sense.

We drove all the way to the movie theater with my mom following right behind. The minute I parked, I braced myself. As I got out, my mom pulled up behind me and rolled down the window. She didn't yell; she was stone-faced and freakishly calm, which was even scarier and more nerve-racking.

"Give the keys to your sister. I'll be back when the movie is over to pick you both up," she said sternly before driving off.

My Best Friend's Wedding will always be the most awful movie I have ever watched because having to sit through it and worry about what awaited me at home tortured me. My mom is a smart lady. She knew that having to sit and develop anxiety over what was coming was far worse than going straight home and taking the punishment.

The following day, in a moment of parental frustration, she said, "I hope you have a child just as crazy as you are."

Wish granted, Mom—times four.

The apple doesn't fall far from the tree, and I've realized in the last few years I'm raising a pack of lying, cheating thieves who will likely form a highly successful crime ring in the coming decades. And one day, I'll be having a police beat conversation of my own.

Every day our home is filled with deceit, from one brother pointing the finger at another when asked who stealth pooped in the laundry basket or all four simply denying they painted the dog with yogurt.

"Mom, a ghost floated into the house, knocked the frame off the wall, and broke it," Teddy once told me, while holding a ball in his guilty little paws. "It was the craziest thing. Too bad it's not on film. We could've sent it to *America's Funniest Home Videos*."

Teddy has explained away many destructive scenes in our house as battle fields.

"I didn't mean to knock over the plant," he has protested. "But Darth Mal was attacking me, and my light saber whipped around and got him."

Another time, shortly after we moved to Texas, one of the boys hid my car keys in a muffin tin and no one was willing to fess up. I ended up having to call my mother-in-law to come over and run everyone to school because I couldn't start my car. Four hours later, after tearing the house apart and wading through coffee grounds, leftover barbecue, and curdled milk in the trash, I found the keys in the baking cabinet.

These are the times when I've had to let go of my

Type A-ness, because I have absolutely no control over maniacal toddlers taking my keys. I've had to take deep breaths and move forward, knowing one day, years later, I will look back and laugh.

For a while, one of their lying tactics was to point the finger at their dad when he was traveling for work.

"Boys, I don't think Daddy flew home at lunch today just to tear apart an entire package of salad mix and sprinkle it throughout the house," I pointed out.

We've had loaves of bread go missing for weeks. My husband recovered his glasses from a bookcase, wedged between a Dr. Seuss book and *Goodnight Moon*. And I once found a handbag I'd been missing for months stashed in the basement, filled with Hot Wheels, rotten baby carrots, and half-eaten Dum-Dums.

As I yell and shake my finger at a lineup of cherry-cheeked, blue-eyed little hellions, I'm reminded that their future life of hardened crime originates in them being smart, curious little boys.

I also realize what goes around comes around when my mom laughs hysterically at the stories of havoc I share. I'm the kid who stuck magnets on the television and sat in awe as it permanently changed colors. I'm also the kid who ran the dishwasher with Dawn instead of detergent and turned our kitchen into a bubble bath.

The damage to your appliances and home is yet another thing they don't go over during parenting preparedness classes. Sure, you learn about how to properly bathe your child or suction the snot out of their nose, but they don't tell you about the cereal bars your child will shove into the DVD player or how he'll take a return address stamp and mark up the couch like he's playing Bingo.

Have babies, they say.

It will enrich your lives, they say.

You know what else it will do? Destroy your house and rack up your credit card charges. At least that's what happens when you have three toddlers who side hustle as bulldozers.

When I was pregnant with my oldest, we hired a baby safety specialist who appeared on *The Oprah Winfrey Show* to come tell us all the ways our home was going to murder our child. Every window blind cord was going to strangle him; the floor vents were sure to amputate a finger. And don't even get me started on the death traps known as our staircases. We accommodated most of the specialist's suggestions because I was a Type A, first-time mom. We covered our fireplace in Plexiglas, locked cabinets, and more. Obviously, as I write this book, my children have all survived the crawling/putting-everything-in-their-mouths phase, but it had little to do with the major safety tactics we put in place.

I'll never forget turning the corner with a large basket of laundry one morning when the triplets were four months old. They were sitting in a row in their little bouncer seats, dozing on and off while *Mickey Mouse Clubhouse* played in the background. My oldest was just shy of four years old and so proud to show me how he had turned his brothers into piggy banks by shoving mouthfuls of pennies and dimes into their slobbery, toothless mouths that had yet to sample solid food. Just rewriting this story gives me the shakes.

On another occasion, he managed to get the dog's leash around one of their necks and play "dog walker" with them. I lost years off my life with that one.

And one sunny spring afternoon, I decided to leave their bedroom window cracked to freshen the room while they napped. While on the phone with my husband moments later, I heard a loud crash and watched in horror as the screen from their second-story nursery window came crashing down onto the patio furniture.

Their heart-stopping antics still shave years off of my life on a weekly basis, and throughout the years of their madness, they've racked up quite a bill for their stay at Chez Cuthbert.

When we found out we were moving to Texas from the Chicago suburbs, we had to bring in a team to fix drywall and paint throughout our home to get it on the market. For most people with normal children, it's a simple crack or ding here or there. But mine legitimately ate the drywall off the corners of the walls in their bedroom. A huge hole gaped in the wall at the bottom of the basement stairs because they threw our ottoman down several times just to "see what would happen."

We had to have bars installed on their nursery bedroom window because once they learned how to pop out the screen, they began shoving books out onto the roof and attempting dance parties for the entire neighborhood to witness. Three DVD players, countless lamps, two flat-screen televisions, two seatbelts in my car —the list goes on forever. One unnamed child cut open the leather seats of my husband's car with one of those tools you use in case of an emergency. Another unscrewed all of the knobs on my hutch and they've never been recovered. They also messed with the water spigot so badly that the day we were leaving town for the Fourth of July we couldn't shut off the water and had to call an emergency plumber.

Do you hear a crackling sound in your head while reading this? Do you smell the smoke and feel the heat of our money constantly going up in flames? Because that's exactly what happened for years. Hell, it's still happening. Not even a month into our new home one broke the pricy pool sweep and another etched designs into our kitchen tile with a fork. It's embarrassing to bring in my car for a wash because my kids treat it like their own personal trash can. There are M&M's and Pirate's Booty shoved so deeply down into some crevasses, not even the deepest of detailed cleanings can remove them.

One day, as Mark and I attempted to sit down and prepare a financial budget for the year, we included the line item of "Cuthbert Boys' Hotel Stay": a running tally of the cost of their destruction. We joke that we'll hand it to them when they turn 18 and they can begin paying it off, but in reality, it's the price of raising little hellions. My husband tries to get me to distinguish between damage caused by boys having fun, boys being curious, boys acting in defiance, or boys embracing pure pandemonium. I've told him time and time again, the lines are blurred beyond belief. So for now, I'll continue to purchase lamps with a six- to 12-month life expectancy and wait until they've flown the coop to invest in anything of true value.

∾

Learning to Laugh Through the Fury

This is one of the most challenging mindsets to accomplish as a mother. A new hole in the drywall, a destroyed kitchen five minutes after I've cleaned it—these are major triggers that send me over the edge into crazy, angry, frustrated mom. I am 100 percent guilty of flying off the handle countless times, and if I could go back, I would do my best to remain calmer in these moments of outrage. Because of my constant visible state of rage, my oldest has developed anxiety over my well-being. Now, anytime we have chaos and I raise my voice or appear stressed and angry, he immediately becomes upset and worried about me, which kills me as a mother. It's not practical to think you won't ever yell or act crazy in front of your kids if they engage in half the shenanigans mine do, but if I have any advice to give, it's try to keep it to a dull roar versus screaming. It's extremely hard to do in the moment, but no one wants the guilt I carry, knowing my outbursts have contributed to my oldest child's anxiety.

So how do you laugh through the fact that a tornado is following you around the house destroying your possessions? Yell and reprimand in comical cartoon voices. Try it; it works. There's something about yelling at them in a Pee Wee Herman voice that magically changes your mood and grabs their attention.

Also, don't beat yourself up if you're having a moment. Sometimes you can't calm down on the spot. Sometimes you need to walk away, find a quiet corner, and chant to yourself, "This too shall pass, and I will eventually look back one day and laugh." Then, take the moment and find some humor in it and share with others. As you post to social media or text a friend, you'll find pity and laughter rolled into one and it will eventually make you laugh as well. Sometimes sharing our frustration with others who relate, can really help us find some semblance of humor. In my mind, it's the definition of grace: taking a situation that would normally make someone cry and learning to laugh at it.

7

LEARNING TOLERANCE

YOU DO YOU, SHIRLEY IN FROZEN FOODS

A few things happen when you go out in public with triplets who happen to be dressed alike and are flipping adorable.

First, people immediately feel like they're at a petting zoo. No joke.

Something comes over them, as if they've just discovered little baby goats and pot-bellied pigs waiting to be plucked out of a field of daisies and swooned over. Strangers pick up, kiss, and pet your children without asking. They take out their phones to snap photos of them, no permission asked.

I truly wouldn't have been surprised if someone had whipped out a boob and tried to feed one of them—that's the degree of mayhem seeing three of a kind provokes in some people. It would have been quite awkward to utter the words, "Cheryl, Karen, and Theresa, please put your Hanes Her Way pushup bras back on. Their bellies are full, and you've become mentally unhinged while in close proximity to triplets. Y'all need to see someone about that."

One of their former preschool teachers routinely asked my children for kisses on the lips, and I had to address it with the administration. She also cut out newspaper photos of my kids and told people they were "her boys," and described her vivid dreams of my being in tears after giving one of my triplets to her to keep. Needless to say, we left that school and never looked back. You can't change crazy, people.

The list of wild encounters we've experienced never ends. My sister and I were once at the park with the triplets when they were about seven months old. Japanese tourists, who had likely never seen a trio of blond-haired, rosy-cheeked babies before, swarmed us as though Jesus himself was standing before them. They flocked us with their cameras like we were the Kardashi-ans, and it was downright frightening. I tried to politely ask them not to pick up my children, but they spoke no English. At one point my sister had to pull a child from a woman's arms like a flat-screen TV at Walmart on Black Friday.

Granted, triplets are not something you see every day, but good Lord, it's not like you just scored a selfie with the Pope. You did not witness the real Tupac buying Cheetos and some Mad Dog 20/20 at the gas station. Three little babies are not on par with a bearded lady in a clown car smoking a peace pipe.

I digress.

Some people are very nice and ask if they can take a photo. Others stick their cellphones out of their car windows while my kids and I walk into Target.

One lady accosted us in the produce aisle and had no shame. She must have been shooting an Instagram Live or something, and it was beyond annoying.

"Mama, why does that lady have her phone on us?" one of my babes asked while we all death stared in her direction.

"I don't know, guys," I replied very loudly. "Apparently she doesn't know how to ask for permission when filming people in the Brussels sprouts section."

It's an awkward circumstance to find yourself in, because on the one hand, I share a ton of photos and stories about my children on social media and, well, in this book. But on the other hand, you can't just allow any Tom, Dick, or "Kinda Scary Larry" to photograph your kids. My husband and I made a rule very early on, when an odd couple at a street art fair stalked our stroller, that we wouldn't allow anyone we didn't know to take photos. Considering we're always on display, it's sometimes awkward to tell the seemingly nice grandma "no," but most people are very understanding.

Sometimes I wish I did have a camera rolling, and that's to catch the look on the faces of passersby who happen to see our crew in action in our front yard.

My husband has countless stories of top executives from his company, who happen to cruise past our house while leisurely strolling through the neighborhood with their spouses. What do they witness?

They see children climbing so high up in the trees they can look into the second-story windows. They see half-naked kids darting out the door, chasing one another with Nerf guns or possibly their forks from dinner. They witness scooter beat-downs and all of the flowers from our bushes being pulled off. And they witness me chasing them down, like the nanny in a Tom and Jerry cartoon.

In those moments, I'm part Ouiser from *Steel Magnolias* and part Madea and Peggy Cleary from *The Kids are Alright*.

It's a stark contrast to the Carol Brady/June Cleaver combo who drops them off at school each morning: polished, put-together with a smile.

The second thing people like to do when witnessing triplets is ask you every detail of your pregnancy and life while also sharing theirs.

Take Shirley, in the frozen foods section at Costco. Ol' Shirl is one example of the same encounter I still experience weekly.

While browsing frozen broccoli she spotted my cart full of plump little babies in matching polos and shorts. It had been a long day, and I really needed to get out of the grocery store and home to make dinner. Shirley immediately approached me with an "Oh my God, am I seeing triple? Are they triplets? Are they all yours?"

First, Shirley, would they all be dressed the same if they weren't mine? Do you think I told the neighbor, "Sure, Kelly, drop your son off and I'll dress him exactly like mine to go to Costco"?

She continued: "Wow. Just wow. Are they natural?"

Define "natural," Shirley. Are they robots? No. Did they grow and come out of my stomach? Yes. They are natural. It's one of the most annoying questions you can ask a mother of multiples, and equally as annoying when people my parents' age ask it casually in the middle of a festival or town gathering. Why complete strangers feel they have any right to ask about the conception of my children is beyond me. Yes, triplets are a rare sighting, but their presence doesn't mean you can start asking for their mother's medical records. Did Shirley want me to give her my OBGYN's phone number so she could learn more?

As my kids started getting restless in the cart while also smashing the bread and eggs, Shirley then began to tell me about how her daughter has two kids a year apart, so she can relate.

Oh, bless your little heart, sweet, sweet Shirl.

There is no universe in which these two experiences are comparable. But I just smiled and said, "Oh, good luck to her," so I could move onto the wine department and get the heck out of the store before my kids required another churro to cooperate.

A dad at my sons' karate class once asked if I breastfed them all. Thanks for making it awkward, Greg.

Another time, my mom's friend whom I do not know posted publicly on Facebook asking all about my IVF journey. Really, Joann?

Others blurt out things that are hurtful without even thinking.

"Ugh, no girls? Not one? Are you going to try for a girl?" I hear this a lot.

If I added one more child to this family I'm pretty sure my husband would be wheeling me off to a looney bin or Betty Ford in the coming years. And oh, by the way, people, boys are pretty awesome, and I love that I have four of them.

"Triple trouble," one man muttered with a disgusted face when he passed us in town. It pissed off my South-side Chicago mother-in-law to the point of needing to fire back.

"I think you meant to say, 'Triple the blessings!'" she yelled.

Should you run into a mom of triplets, or any multiples, assume that, whether they had a fertility journey or not, they went through the ordeal of carrying those babies and bringing them into the world. And the best thing you can do is offer words of encouragement.

"You're doing great, Mama!" is a good one. I also really like, "Keep up the good work! You've got this!"

And if you know a Shirley, tell her to pipe down. If she's that curious about life with multiples, suggest this book.

∼

Learning Tolerance

If you're a mother and have ever gone out in public with your child, I'm guessing there's a 99 percent chance you've experienced some version of sweet Shirley at Costco. Maybe a relative at a holiday gathering asked if you're pregnant when it's just the baby tummy left over from the previous child. Or maybe the random person in line at the grocery store wants to know all the details behind a birthmark on your baby's head.

Sweet readers, there comes a time in life when you realize that not everyone is raised with manners or tact. Some are excited and have no filter, so they ask all the questions they shouldn't. Others are curious and have no boundaries, asking personal information that's really none of their business.

Over time, two things have helped me gain tolerance when dealing with the Shirleys out there. I always start with a smile and answer the first question. If the questioning continues too long, I have a list of kind excuses in my back pocket to use:

"So sorry—can't talk. By the smell of things, this one needs to be changed."

"Oh gosh, I would love to chat, but we're late to pick up my oldest at soccer. Gotta run!"

At the end of the day, 99 percent of Shirleys mean no ill will, so I try my best to not show my irritation when asked probing, inappropriate questions. Larry at the Whole Foods meat counter really doesn't need to know if my birth was natural, but I just smile and say, "Sure was! Now how about those filet mignons?"

Finding tolerance with curious strangers can also bring more laughter and joy to your experience, because while you're left shaking your head with disbelief at their questions, retelling their absurdity to friends and family will surely have you all cracking up.

8

LEARNING PATIENCE

LIFE IS A FRAT HOUSE, AND WE'RE THE CAMPUS POLICE

The year was 2003, and I was a week away from graduating college. The warm summer nights had begun in Chico, California, and my friends and I were walking home arm in arm from what would be our final fraternity party.

Or so I thought.

For a while, my life did resemble a grownup's. I traveled around Europe, ate at fancy restaurants, and attended galas in prestigious art museums. I bought a suit and went on job interviews. I was adulting hard. But little did I know that having four boys in a span of three-and-a-half years would bring me right back to that fraternity house, complete with holes punched in the walls, underwear flung on the ceiling fan, and the same horrible hangover, only this time from lack of sleep instead of crappy keg beer.

Raising triplet toddlers is like the biggest college party you've ever attended, including the cleanup the following morning. Half-finished drinks litter the lawn, the floors are always sticky, and someone constantly stumbles down the hallway naked or bangs on the door when you're trying to pee. I walk into the TV room to find Cartoon Network blaring as four, half-dressed boys stare at the screen looking dazed and confused, which reminds me of most Sunday mornings when I used to swing by to visit one of my fraternity friends. In college, I sometimes spent Saturday nights sitting on the roof of my friends' fraternity house with beer and a BB gun, trying to catch the neighborhood raccoon who kept tearing up their trash cans. Nowadays, the boys and I hide out in our pajamas with a squirt bottle, waiting to scare the squirrel who keeps raiding our bird feeder. So many similarities, right?

Like other fraternity brothers, the Cuthbert boys are constantly in some sort of competitive state, cheering, chanting, and egging on one another to do something incredibly stupid. One week, I found them attempting to pet our then senile, grouchy dachshund to see whose fingers she would nip first. (R.I.P. Fergi Cuthbert, 2004–2018. You put up with a lot of crap from those boys. There's a special place in dog heaven for you.)

When they're not busy "double dog daring" each other, they're taking partying to a whole new level: climbing trees so high they're staring me straight in the eyes through the second-story window. They have a fondness for streaking and spanking each other with anything that resembles a paddle, and they've never met a piece of cold, next-day pizza they didn't like.

Partying aside, my boys also share a strong bond with one another like so many fraternity members do, and they always have one another's backs.

Watching them at the park when someone attempts to bully one of them is like actively participating in a sociological experiment. They can pick on each other until the cows come home, but if someone outside of their little pack tries to throw some shade, look out— because their posse will take down an outsider like Kung Fu ninja masters.

As I go through the motions of cleaning up the wreckage from living in a fraternity house, I try to keep the mess in perspective. I silently mouth a ton of curse words to dissipate the anger of once again wiping pudding off the wall or stepping on yet another LEGO, but at the same time, I try to remind myself how wonderful it is that I get to be here for this. While staying home with my kids is tough, and I sometimes wish I had chosen a career instead of carpools and cartoons, having a traveling spouse often reminds you of how good you have it.

Yes, the days are long when you stay home, but you're there for the little moments. Each day when my oldest was in kindergarten the bus would come pick him up at noon. All four boys would finish lunch, and we'd spend a good 15 minutes out on the front porch together, just talking about what excites us at the moment. Sometimes it was Mickey Mouse or yogurt-covered raisins, and other times it was the leaves turning or the first snowfall of the year. These little conversations have stayed in my memory far longer than the elaborate family outings and events I've planned.

While the constant meltdowns may make my eye twitch, it's the special little moments, like toasting with my morning coffee and their milk sippies, that will last. I'm happy I could be there to experience them.

In the early years of our chaos, my husband traveled for work up to four days a week. I'm sure there were Monday mornings he couldn't wait to jump on a plane, because three 18-month-olds can seem like a picnic full of crap sandwiches at times. I was just reminding him of the time the triplets had the runs for 10 days, and he didn't have a single memory of it, so needless to say, travel can help your mental health in a big way when raising multiples.

Very early on, because he was always on the road, my

husband decided he didn't want to be the disciplinarian in our house. Because his time at home was limited, in his mind he should spend it having fun with our kids, not disciplining them.

"I'm home so little that when I am, I don't want to spend my time with them yelling and disciplining them," he said. "I just want to have fun. Just think of me as Santa Claus."

The problem with being the "fun parent" is when you do need to lay down the law from time to time, no one listens.

After a long, hot summer day when the triplets were two, I laughed until I cried watching Mark try to command his troops.

We had tucked Tommy, Teddy, and Nate into bed and just after we shut the door, we heard them scampering about. Considering that during the month prior they had snuck all sorts of toddler contraband into their room, like permanent markers, ketchup packets, and hairspray, we knew this wasn't a good sign.

Exhausted, I asked my husband to go in and give them a stern talking to.

He did.

And they laughed.

"Let me show you how the professionals do it," I said, as I prepared my bad cop voice.

"Get back in your beds right now or I'm taking your pillows and sheets and you can sleep on the floor like farm animals!" I shouted, sounding like a burly, angry drill sergeant.

Within seconds of seeing my crazy eyes, they sprinted back into their beds like little cockroaches. We didn't hear another peep out of them the rest of the night. My husband was impressed with my power, but I reminded him, he's the one that gave it to me.

Back then, I was jealous of his superhero status, but on that hot summer night, I realized I have the best of both roles.

Sure, I've given more timeouts, mommy death stares, and "take your butt off your brother's head" directives than I can count. I've reprimanded back talk and hauled a 50-pound kid up a flight of stairs as he kicked and screamed.

Yes, I break up fist fights, but I also receive unconditional love and hugs every day. A "talking to" always ends with a kiss on the cheek and an "I love you," something Santa Claus Mark only got on the weekends. When your spouse travels, it's easy to get disgruntled that they're not there to help or experience children crawling up their legs. But you have to empathize with the fact that when there are good days—and there are many—your spouse has to hear about them over the phone or FaceTime instead of in the moment with you. When something funny happens, they don't get to laugh along with everyone else; they just hear about it later.

The idea that the grass is always greener can even apply to parenting roles sometimes. While the day-today can often seem ordinary or mundane, there are little moments of beauty too. Sticking out the head-butts to witness the tender moments makes it all worth it.

As I attempt to clean up their wreckage and keep our home from completely losing all its value on a daily basis, I try to remind myself that this too shall pass. I search for ear plugs on Amazon to block out their deafening volume, realizing one day the noise will be replaced with lonely quiet. And in a decade I'll replace the carpet and no longer have to face the judging eyes of the Stanley Steamer carpet cleaner guys.

∿

Learning Patience

Prior to having children, my nickname from my husband was "No Patience McGee" because I always sprinted to the next thing at race car speed. If we went out for drinks with friends, I'd be ready to hit the next bar halfway through the first pint. I've always felt a strong sense of urgency within me, and that characteristic pairs with very little natural patience.

I wish I could sit here and tell all moms of littles that this phase will pass and eventually you won't be ready to blow smoke out of your ears on any given afternoon. The problem with that advice is, it's a bold-faced lie. As I sit here writing this book, some child of mine, well out of diapers and preschool, has driven his toy up the walls to our playroom, making tire marks along the fresh paint. Another just had a meltdown because he requested a warm hotdog for lunch but changed his mind and now wants it cold. According to him, I'm the meanest mom on the planet for not just giving him another hot dog.

St. Francis de Sales once said, "Have patience with all things, but first of all with yourself."

These are words to live by for moms trying to manage it all. We try to be patient with the chaos happening around us and then we get angry with ourselves for yelling or flipping out. While we need to strive to let go of the frustration that comes with raising tiny humans, we also need to be patient with our own emotions. I am constantly reminding myself that the expectations on moms today are unattainable in many ways, and to keep my sanity, I must let go of some of the aftermath of raising destructive little boys. The marker on our dining room chair, for example, is a great conversation starter at dinner parties. Holding onto the frustration I feel when one creates an "experiment" with food coloring that ends up on my white cabinets, will only fester into anger and outrage. As you focus on trying to turn a blind eye to the ruin around you, also be patient with your own reactions. We are human. It's human nature to lose your mind when faced with an unruly child who loves to test your patience.

9

LEARNING TO REWRITE SCRIPTS

LIFE IS ONE BIG SKETCH COMEDY

They say that everyone has a script in life. For example, my mom's is a Garry Marshall holiday rom-com. In the movie that plays out in her head, my sister, brother, and I show up with our spouses and kids and all pile into her home for Christmas. Her grandchildren, all in plaid pajamas that also match her dog's outfit, curl up together by the tree and sip hot cocoa while bonding over a Christmas classic like *Home Alone*. She hovers in the kitchen, preparing gingerbread houses to decorate while a Balsam Fir candle from Bath and Body Works sets the wintery mood. Hilarious shenanigans ensue, and we share in holiday cheer.

A lifetime of cute "remember whens" roll into our family's playbook. Think *National Lampoon's Christmas Vacation* meets *The Family Stone* meets The Hallmark Channel but without anyone being sick and dying. The closest we've ever come to these kinds of shenanigans was Thanksgiving of 2017, when my dad sneezed with a mouth full of wine, dousing my brother-in-law with Cabernet Sauvignon mid-meal. My husband still cries laughing when the story is recalled.

Anyway, where were we? Oh yes, my mom's script.

You can imagine that with this image and life goal in her mind, it completely rocked her world when we decided to start staying home for Christmas instead of traveling to California. We wanted our kids to wake up on Christmas morning in their own home, and the idea of hauling gifts through the airport during the busiest time of year to travel gave me the shakes.

This decision changed the screenplay in her movie of life, and as my boys grow older, I'm realizing I need to adjust my own as well.

I always dreamed of sharing my childhood experiences with my kids and watching the excitement in their eyes as I told of the amazingness of the '80s. I believed they would be wowed by my adventures of rollerblading to 7-11 with my bestie and walking to the wharf to feed the sea lions.

"There was even a monkey who kissed your hand if you gave him a penny!" I said with amazement, knowing damn well these monkeys were probably put out of business by PETA years ago.

During a recent trip to California, I began a monologue while my kids were sharing donuts in the exact place my grandpa took me as a kid. I had all the nostalgic feels. Red's Donuts on Alvarado Street in Downtown Monterey hasn't changed a bit since I was five years old, sneaking sips of my grandpa's coffee. I was halfway through a story about a childhood visit there when one of my kids interrupted me: "Uhhhh, Mom? Which do you think is faster: a jet plane or a propeller plane?"

For the love of all that's holy, here I was thinking I was sharing some special moment in time, a story they would cherish for years, and their minds were completely elsewhere. This happens to me constantly with my kids. They'll ask an important question in the car, and the opportunity for an incredible life lesson presents itself—a teachable moment, if you will. And instead of just muttering "uh huh," like I do after many of their queries, I choose to try to teach them something.

One day, my oldest climbed in the car, telling me all about his school friend's rich dad who drives a Ferrari.

"He is super rich and gets to go to all the professional sports games," he said. "Are we rich? How come I can't do that? It's not fair."

This is the moment! I thought. *I will sear into their brains that we don't discuss money with people because it's obnoxious and frankly doesn't matter. I will teach them that discussing how much we have can often make others feel uncomfortable and talking about it does no good. I will tell them we are not rich, but we are blessed to have everything we need: food on our table, a roof over our heads, and each other.*

As I climbed on my soap box and began my monologue, the exact same thing happened as in the donut shop.

"Mom, what's at the center of the earth? Is it really lava? Are volcanos like pimples on the earth?" one child probed in a series of rapid-fire questions. The entire conversation changed to magma and tectonic plates, and my prolific parenting moment vanished. Observing the thought processes of little boys is a lot like a watching a cat following a laser pointer. Their minds are all over the place, bouncing from one thought to another.

"Mom, is a burp really just a fart that comes out of your mouth?" one asked as I was explaining the meaning of Easter.

The list goes on for days.

When all four boys are involved in some deep retelling of a story to their dad, my quietest one, who just wants to be a part it all, chimes in with something totally off the wall like, "Waffles!" And just like that, suddenly they're discussing how they like their waffles with extra butter, syrup, and Nutella, even though 60 seconds prior they were fixated on soccer and the solar system.

Changing my script has meant accepting that many days will just be ordinary and mundane. I've learned to appreciate those. Those are good, calm days, and if you look hard enough, they host their own special little moments. It's also meant accepting that sometimes they will care about my past, and other times they won't.

For example, they randomly love hearing stories about my great-aunt Mary, who died decades before they were born. They love that she was feisty, had whiskers, and always smelled like coffee.

But they couldn't care less about the mementos I kept from childhood for my one-day children.

Recently, after a massive household purge (thanks to Marie Kondo's *Tidying Up* on Netflix), I gave away my high school cheerleading pompoms to Goodwill. Those crinkly balls of Mylar strips brought so much immense joy to my life, but no one in my house wants them, and they've collected dust in the corner of my closet. And by the time I potentially have a granddaughter one day, my pompoms will be relics and probably in the early stages of decomposition. At one point, I gave the boys my Trolls collection, and they scalped them. I kept finding hairless Troll Dolls all over the house. Then one night, one of my boys took them all and made a Trolls shrine in the window by his bed.

Am I raising toy deviants or what? Those poor Trolls.

As a Type A mama, scripts have always been an

important part of my functionality. And up until I had my boys I always relied on them. But with scripts come high expectations and inevitable letdown and disappointment. So while I still have goals for our family in the future, I leave the plot twists and turns up to God and know it will all pan out the way it's meant to be.

~

Learning to Rewrite Scripts

My husband was born and raised in the Chicago area, and when we married we always knew we'd eventually move back there. Early in our relationship we lived in California, Tennessee, and Boston, and having grown up in a small town, I always knew I wanted to plant some roots somewhere permanently and raise a family.

In 2008, we did just that and bought a home in a small, beautiful Chicago community while investing ourselves in different charities and organizations. I truly believed this was it for us. My friends and I joked about one day getting on the wait list at the old folks' home there and sharing afternoon cocktails while wearing hot pink lipstick and bedazzled sweaters.

Eight years later, we got the shock of our lives when a job offer in Texas was too good to be true. The company offered my husband the job on a Friday, and that Sunday my mother-in-law and I hopped on a plane to look for houses. I was in complete shock and disbelief. My mother-in-law and I went to dinner after a long day of looking at homes and I just cried uncontrollably, like you do when you grieve.

This move was not in my script, and it threw me hard.

Once the move was made and time passed, I realized that while I miss Chicago, moving to Texas was one of the greatest things to ever happen to our family.

Rewriting your script so it's more of an editable outline can help ease a lot of motherhood anxiety. The script God has for us is more like improv comedy because just when you think you've got everything figured out, life has a way of surprising you. Learning to roll with the ebbs and flows makes the journey so much more enjoyable.

10

LEARNING TO NOT REFEREE

SNITCHES GET STITCHES: A NON-PC GUIDE TO RAISING
PROBLEM SOLVERS

6:53 A.M. "Maaaaama! John told me I smell."

6:54 A.M. "Maaaah! Nate said I'm adopted!"

7:01 A.M. "Mama, Tommy hurt my feelings."

7:02 A.M. "Mooooom, Teddy won't stop looking at me."

On an average morning in my home, all of this chatter and ridiculous tattling occurs before the coffee has even been poured.

"Boys, I am not a referee. Don't come to me to figure out your problems," I scold while examining the latest wrinkle they've produced on my forehead. "Talk with your brothers and work it out. This is life, guys. No one is going to solve all your problems for you."

Before I delve into my no-nonsense form of child rearing, let me assure you that while I'm not the "let's sit and explore our emotions" mom by trade, my boys know they're extremely loved and are happy, joyful little souls. They are also resilient, grit-developing, and confident—things they'll desperately need in this changing world.

That may mean that sometimes they resolve altercations with a karate chop to the leg and then a full-fledged headlock and noogie instead of mindful mediation. But after the dust has settled, they hug it out, say "I love you," and return to riding scooters together in the front yard.

They may bicker and interrupt each other, but their love is deep and fierce. Once in a McDonald's Play Place, some boys were picking on one of my triplets, who was only two at the time. Their big brother, without any prompting, swooped in to defend his brother. We wound up at urgent care for stitches in his lip as a result of the bully's fist, but needless to say, I was proud of his protective instinct.

The motto in our house of boys is "snitches get stitches," a term that may frighten some who lean toward the overly nurturing side of parenting. But for a house with four boys ages eight and under, it's a survival motto that teaches them valuable life skills.

First, they need to be able to problem solve. They are growing up in an era in which a quick Google search gives them all the information they need. It's a wonderful time to be alive, but it's also crippling to kids' ability to be creative, strategic thinkers. For example, I chose to stop umpiring their constant fight about who is allowed in one another's bedrooms. Consequently, they came up with their own rules of bartering toys and offering lavish promises for entry. It means less refereeing for me, and more negotiating, bargaining, and establishing real-world social skills for them. They've also watched me plug a bloody nose so many times that now, when they wrestle and someone receives a punch to the face, they transform into little medics and help each other out before calling for help.

Second, they need to learn loyalty, even if that means harmlessly sneaking behind my back. No one likes a tattletale, and my rule is unless someone is bleeding and needs to go to urgent care or could potentially be harmed, I don't need to know about it. If they've managed to sneak a bag of mini marshmallows up to their room without me noticing, kudos to them for their stealth skills. But if one of them comes to tattle, the entire operation is busted.

This is where the type A in me has had to ease up. When I discover piles of tiny, balled-up foil chocolate wrappers in a guest bedroom, I'm annoyed they got into the Easter candy, but I'm also proud they pulled off sneaking away with it.

Finally, they need to learn time and place and minding their own business in an appropriate manner, another skill set that will help them a ton when navigating adult relationships. When I was a kid, we didn't dare interrupt our parents when they were speaking with other adults. These days, my kids want to hang during girls' nights and will eavesdrop and attempt to chime in on adult discussions.

"Mom, Mrs. Smith's girls' trip on the coast sounded like sooooo much fun," one kid, who was hiding in the stairwell on wine night, chirped with a smile. "Did they ever find their friend after the booze cruise?"

In a changing world of technology and social norms, the things we worry about as parents and prepare our kids for are constantly evolving. Like any other parent, I will inevitably screw up a million times over in attempting to raise good human beings. But rest assured, they will be confident, loyal, and able to MacGyver their way out of situations, hopefully without too many stitches along the way.

∾

Learning Not to Referee

Have you ever been on a playdate with your child and every five to 10 minutes another child comes up to tattle about something yours has done?

You and the other mom have now spent 30 minutes

attempting to get through a three-minute story or conversation because every 45 seconds some child says, "He looked at me wrong," or, "She's not sharing."

When kids are really young, I think it's important to remind them of the proper response to situations, but at a certain age, it's time for them to start handling their own problems. When my son comes home from school and says a classmate's been mean to him, I don't call the teacher and ask her to handle it. Instead, I teach my son how to have a conversation with the other student and figure out why he's not being nice.

Obviously, sometimes as a parent you need to get involved. But when it comes to everyday arguments among siblings, learning not to referee their grievances will help them become more self-sufficient in the future. In my opinion, if they're helpless in solving a simple dispute over who gets to choose which show to watch, how will they learn the skills necessary to talk things out as adults?

Learning not to referee is simple. Assess the situation at hand. Is it a big problem, like your child is hurt, or is it a small problem, like someone looked at them wrong? When they do come to tattle, remind them of how smart and capable they are of handling the situation themselves. Turn not tattling into a positive.

Studies show that anxiety, depression, and lack of coping skills are on the rise in our children today. How are we, as parents, contributing to their inability to handle emotions and conflict?

11

LEARNING TO EMBRACE THE NASTY

THE TRASH CAN ON WHEELS

Anyone who grew up watching *Saturday Night Live* in the '90s remembers Adam Sandler's famous song, "Piece-of-(Bleep) Car." It was all about Adam's broke-down ride, which sported a cracked windshield and busted seatbelt he had to tie into place.

I hum this song each time a friend gets in to carpool with me, because it breaks the ice on how completely disgusting the interior of my car is. It's my way of learning to laugh at a nasty situation that is completely out of my control. I do the best to stay on top of the episode of *Food Hoarders* happening inside my car, even keeping a vacuum inside the garage for constant cleanouts. But it never lasts long.

I'm fortunate that the main mechanics in my beat-to-hell 2011 Buick Enclave still function, but not much else does. It's a stark contrast to my cars prior to children, which were meticulously washed on pay day and had a perfectly organized CD case. The Type A in me even stored Armor All wipes in the glove compartment, but nowadays you're more likely to find *Scooby-Doo* DVDs and wrappers containing half-eaten lollipops.

That's the price a vehicle pays when carting around four boys countless hours a day. The seat warmers no longer work, and one of the reverse lights no one can quite seem to replace. My children have busted off almost every knob and dial, and the crumbs are so deep they've become part of the car. The pieces of cosmetic plastic that hide the metal hardware under the seats have been ripped off by little, barbaric hands.

Each time my children step foot inside, it's as if they hold a sledge hammer in one hand and a fist full of fruit snacks in the other, ready to demolish anything they see while their heads swivel in circles.

One time I thought it would be safe to give my boys chocolate milkshakes in the car. It was during the dead heat of summer, and they had to run a million not-so-fun errands with me that day—think flooring store and the post office. They were less than pleased but had behaved thus far, so on that sweaty, armpit stain of a July afternoon, I swung by a drive-thru for a tasty, ice-cold reward.

"Two hands, people! Two hands!" I yelled as I passed back the milkshakes.

Just as we pulled out of the parking lot, the inevitable happened. One dropped his shake in the third row. As it plummeted to the car floor, it splashed up on the brother sitting to his left, causing him to blow a gasket. A ruckus then ensued, forcing the second milkshake to fly across the car and hit the window.

"For the love of all that's holy, what the heck is going on back there?!" I yelled while trying to navigate merging onto the frontage road.

By the time we reached home 10 minutes later, it was like a Willy Wonka crime scene in my car, like Augustus Gloop himself had enjoyed an epic binge up in the back of my Buick.

A disaster of this proportion can't simply be cleaned with a wipe-down and dust buster. No, ma'am. Those milkshakes had worked their way into every crack and crevasse in my vehicle, and in the hot Texas sun, that milk was about to get really rank, really fast.

We often joke that once you have kids, each family typically has one nice car, which belongs to Dad, and one trash can on wheels, also known as the Mom Wagon. Whether it's Hatchimals that wind up in the wheel grooves of the middle row captain's chair or a juice box completely emptied into a cup holder that you don't notice for a week, the Mom Wagon is a whole new level of grotesque.

Today's moms are constantly on the go much more than our own mothers ever were. The worst thing my mom had to deal with was a McDonald's ice cream cone brushing the ceiling when she took a speed bump too fast. These days my children have no choice but to eat multiple meals and snacks in the car weekly. When we're running late to school, they take muffins to go, slinging them all over my car like shotputs. And the last time we were stuck in traffic on our way to hockey practice, someone thought it would be fun to smash McDonald's BBQ sauce packets on the back seat. My car's aroma will never be the same, despite multiple efforts to clean it. Combine the smell of the sauce with stinky sneakers and you'll understand why I drive with the windows down even in the rain.

One of my girlfriends found a half-eaten applesauce pouch in her car, left for dead like roadkill. It molded her car so badly, even a detailing couldn't get it out. Another accidentally left her car window down a crack, and a squirrel came in and helped itself to all of the car snacks and a half-zipped lunch box. That squirrel had the time of its furry life! When the family returned to their car, the squirrel was still busy eating. He and the mom equally scared one another, and he pounced right onto her chest, attempting to flee. Since that day, the squirrel and Sara have never been the same.

My trusty Enclave has now surpassed the 100,000-mile mark, and I've been toying with the idea of finally buying a new car. But taking my car for a wash and vacuum each week reminds me why I should wait, because about five miles after we've pulled out of the wash, new mystery goo appears on the windows and a booger is wiped on the back of the driver's headrest.

I've had to accept that, for now, I'll spend half of my day shuffling kids around like Oscar the Grouch in my six-cylinder trash receptacle. And I'll continue to give my steering wheel a high-five daily, thanking my old car for tolerating the stank and still getting us where we need to go, despite the barf-worthy shape it's in.

∾

Learning to Embrace the Nasty

When this piece of writing first ran on The Today Show's *Facebook page, several people proclaimed their children never make messes in the car and know how to eat properly. Well done, perfect parents hiding behind a computer! I'm so happy for you that your children act so civilized. Despite my best efforts, mine still eat like ravaged wild hogs, so dealing with the disgust of my car is my cross to bear, I suppose.*

Learning to embrace the nasty comes in all forms. The boogers wiped on the shirt, the skid marks, the carrots left in the lunchbox all summer that eventually look like furry hamsters...these are all included in the same category. Parenthood is beautiful but also incredibly disgusting at times.

Should you be raising messy kids like mine, keep a vacuum handy or wash your car weekly just to keep your sanity. And to lift your mood, position an air freshener close to the driver's seat so you can escape the rank smell of sneakers.

12

LEARNING TO STAND YOUR GROUND

FROM STAR CHARTS TO SAN QUENTIN

"**Y**ou have until the count of three to drop your brother out of the headlock and resume peace," I yell.

The countdown is one of several disciplinary tactics many of us parents use to keep our kids in line. My mom often tried this one on us with a liberal approach. Growing up, nothing about my mom was hard-nosed. I only heard her drop an F-bomb one time during my childhood, when the cat jumped up on the dinner table and knocked over an entire gallon of milk. It was probably the final straw in a string of events that took place that day.

When my mom sent us to our rooms, we were back outside playing in 30 minutes, let out by our dad, who was oblivious as to why we were in trouble.

My parents were great communicators. Just kidding.

While my mom had a soft heart and was somewhat of a pushover with standing her ground, my dad was ruthless. I despised mushrooms as a kid and still do. The slimy consistency in my mouth always felt like I was eating slugs and would instantly provoke my gag reflex. And because my dad is Swiss-Italian, almost every meal he made was laced with them. Sunday night family dinners meant I was not allowed to leave the table until my chicken marsala, covered in mushrooms, was eaten. I would scoot them to the side and smear them around and yet was still required to eat them. My father even includes mushrooms in his spaghetti sauce, for the love of God! This man was trying to play parenthood mind games on me at seven-years-old!

I distinctly remember sitting at the dinner table, staring at my mushroom-inundated food, while my sister and brother, who had finished their meals, roller skated in front of the house. The entire table was cleared except for my plate, and my mom passed by while wiping things down and whispered, "Just eat them, honey. Plug your nose and eat them and then you can go play." It's the same line I now tell my oldest about broccoli and anything else green. My Type A drive and inability to back down were not about to surrender to the dinner line my dad drew in the sand. No way.

Over time, I devised a plan that basically involved sitting there until *60 Minutes* was about to come on TV at 7:00 P.M. I distracted with, "Dad, your show is starting," and quickly slipped back into my bedroom, where a shoebox of Red Vines and Nilla wafers awaited.

My dad worked long hours during the week, so we only had to deal with the iron dinner fist on the weekends. During the week, we suffered my mom's threat of a countdown that went a little something like this: "One... two...two-and-a-half...two-and-three-quarters...two-and-four-fifths..."

I've always wondered why she let us go on longer. Maybe it was easier, or maybe she just didn't want to deal with the situation. We've all been there. It's so much easier to let the iPad run out of battery than to take it away, knowing the tantrum that will ensue. Sometimes we truly don't have the energy to put up the fight that is often required in good discipline. When the triplets were toddlers, I would often put them in time-out at the foot of the stairs. This attempt did me no good, because they would sit there screaming bloody murder, and eventually, the other two boys would join in solidarity.

I've sent them to their rooms for time-outs, which works now that they're older, but when they were little, led to full-blown destruction of their rooms. They ripped bedding off the mattresses, broke window blinds—you name it. It was as if the running of the bulls had taken place in the nursery.

I've read a lot of books about disciplining your kids, and they all have great ideas. But here's the thing: when you have this many kids, it's impossible to implement most of the ideas.

When my triplets had just turned three, they became a lot more interested in their big brother's toys and activities. Unlike the triplets, John has always taken care of his things, and his younger brothers' newfound interest in touching his toys created constant fights. At one point he even lassoed them up together like a bunch of goats. I tried group hugs. I brought them in together tight like a coach would with his team. We discussed respecting one another's property. Nothing worked, and they still fight constantly over the same stuff.

A friend suggested a book about sibling fights that she found life-changing. So excited for the possibility of calming the daily brawls down to a simmer, I immediately ordered it and took it along on a flight the following week. Shortly after takeoff, I cracked the book open. Not even two chapters in, I realized there was no chance in hell this book would help my family. The idea was that each time your children fight, you sit them both down and discuss the emotions behind it all. People, if I attempted to do this each time my kids squabbled, I would spend my entire day sitting and discussing feelings. I may as well become a licensed therapist and open a practice in my kitchen. With four kids, there is no time to delve into emotions every single time there is a behavioral flare-up. I can't stop in the middle of Target when they're drop-kicking each other, knocking down an entire display of Valentine's cookies, and talk about why they're angry. There are not enough hours in the day, and there's a 95 percent chance they would tune me out anyway because as soon as I spoke they would focus on trying to convince me to buy the cookies they just knocked over.

Sometimes kids just act out or engage in dumb shenanigans because they're young and impulsive. It's not always linked to some deep-rooted emotion. Sometimes they just feel like pushing their brother into the freezer at Costco to see how he will react.

Two things help me manage some sense of control over my kids' behavior.

The first is star charts. I publicly display them on the laundry room door, and I give out stickers for good behavior and listening skills. The concept is simple: earn a certain number of stars, and you get a prize. It could be something as simple as a LEGO mini figure or an ice cream cone date with me. My children are exceptional opportunists without even knowing it. They'll often try to spin a story in an attempt to get even more out of the star reward.

"Mom, I have the best idea," Teddy says. "What about while we're out getting the ice cream cone, we can swing by Six Flags? I will swap the LEGO guy for some Six Flags rides."

I really can't wait to see his future sales career. It's going to be amazing.

The thing with the star charts is that when my kids act like wild animals, I take away stars. The chart has the ability to be positive and negative reinforcement in one. And when the chart's effect wears off, my husband and I just go for the jugular. What in their lives will they miss the most? What can we threaten to take away that will actually motivate them to amend their behavior? Sports equipment, lovies, iPads, and scooters are all fair game and have been used to manipulate and correct their actions.

The other option isn't as fun. The other part of disciplining four boys that actually works is to stand our ground. It's torturous at times, but necessary. It often ruins fun family outings and can be embarrassing at an event, when we haul one out to the car kicking and screaming. I've planned super fun days with my boys and had one child act up and refuse to listen after multiple threats, causing that one to be left home with Grandma or, worse, resulting in a fun day canceled for everyone.

On one particular occasion, it took everything in my being to stay calm. I took the triplets to Hobby Lobby to pick out some fun craft paper to practice their cutting skills. One of my triplets—the biggest emotional manipulator out of the group—became agitated by something and turned into a sassy teenager in about five seconds. I refused to buy him a toy he'd found, and instead of accepting "no" as an answer, he first argued and then threw a holy fit in the middle of the store, screaming, "You never get me anything! You're the worst mom ever!" The public display quickly caused this Type A control freak to lose her mind. At this point everyone in the store stared as he kicked and screamed and ran away from me. Fed up with embarrassment, I grabbed him by the arm and began leading him out of the store. This is when I wanted to crawl in a hole and hide. As I clutched his arm and sternly guided him out of Hobby Lobby, he began screaming at the top of his lungs, "YOU'RE HURTING ME! STOP HURTING ME! YOU'RE THE WORST MOM EVER AND YOU'RE HURTING ME! I DIDN'T DO ANYTHING WRONG! STOP HURTING ME!"

Every single set of mom eyes in that store were laser focused on our shit show of an exit. I was mortified. I started sweating, turned beet red, and wanted to bolt out the door.

That day, it took everything in me not to stick that child on a street corner with a for sale sign. But then I thought back to a story a group of old guys having coffee on an early morning at McDonald's once told me...

During the summertime when we're at our lake house and have company staying with us, I often take the triplets to McDonalds at 6:00 A.M. They play and eat hot cakes while I sit and enjoy coffee, knowing we aren't waking up anyone in the house. Our lake house is in a tiny town without a Starbucks or Target, so McDonald's is somewhat of an early morning watering hole. Each weekend, there is a group of men well into their 70s and 80s who sit and have coffee. They marvel at my boys running around in their jammies, as triplets are a rare sighting in such a small town. They once told me of a local woman who'd had triplets decades back and one day couldn't deal with them anymore. She dropped them on someone's front porch with a note that read, "Good luck." The story was front page news at the time.

In that moment at Hobby Lobby, with my child making such a scene, I completely understood that woman's desire to throw in the towel. It's moments like that when you feel completely defeated as a parent. You're embarrassed by your child's behavior and hurt that they would treat you like this, and you just want to call it a day.

I hate those kinds of days. But I refuse to allow my children to be disrespectful or disrespect my and their dad's authority. I love nothing more than to have fun and play with my boys, but I'm not their friend right now; I'm the person responsible for raising them right. When they're adults, I will love every second of being their friend, but for now, I have a bigger responsibility on my hands: to make sure they grow into good people.

~

Learning to Stand Your Ground

Disciplining our children is one of the hardest parts of motherhood. Everyone has their own way of doing it, and I'm not here to say my approach is best. Each family has its own dynamics and household culture.

What I will say, is whatever method works for your family, stick to it. Don't bend. Don't announce a rule or a punishment and then back down. When we do this, we demonstrate to our kids that the rules don't always apply. We weaken our own authoritative role, and we also set up our kids to feel entitlement later in life. If we, as parents, don't hold true to our rules and our children accountable for their actions, how will they be as teenagers or adults? Will they then think the rules don't apply to them?

While it's difficult to sit through the meltdown that comes with a punishment, in a way you're setting up your children to be accountable adults later in life. You're building integrity and important character.

When I was having trouble with one kid's behavior a few years back, a therapist told me, "You're far better off holding him accountable now at six or seven than dealing with the repercussions of letting it slide. A young kid who is defiant is much easier to deal with than a teenager with the same issues."

13

LEARNING TO IGNORE JUDGMENT

DEAR BRITTANY AT REGISTER SIX

During the summer of 2017, in the midst of the sweltering San Antonio heat, my family and I moved down to Texas from Chicago. The stress of moving into a new home, registering at new schools, worrying about an approaching hurricane, and then dealing with a gas shortage, was enough to make me hide in my wine cellar while pondering Betty Ford and binge-eating malt balls.

Anyone who has embarked on a cross-country move knows, the first few weeks are filled with frustrating calls to utility companies and countless trips to big box stores to load up on household essentials. I was on one of many Target visits when, unfortunately, a bright-eyed, 22-year-old studying childhood education tried to offer me parenting advice at the worst possible moment.

As I stood at the register with a cart overflowing with paper towels, Lysol wipes, and laundry detergent, my boys were scampering about, poking things on the shelves, and tackling each other.

Yes, I said tackling each other. Because what else do four boys do while waiting for their mom to pay?

Brittany, we'll call her, was in line right behind me with her face wash, tank top, and protein bars. As she watched my typical chaos ensue, she couldn't help but insert her thoughts on discipline as she heard me yell at my oldest to stop pants-ing his brother for the fourth time.

"So I find that if you go down to their level, speak in a really calm, quiet voice, and ask them what feelings are making them act this way, you'll be amazed at the difference in behavior," she said with a big smile, as if she had just bestowed upon me this huge parenting hack. "They're really just acting out because they want their emotions heard."

Her face in that moment beamed. She had probably learned this amazing discipline technique from an early childhood education class lecture or textbook and felt so excited to share it with this poor mother attempting to wrangle her unruly children.

The cashier and I locked eyes, sharing a "you've got to be kidding" expression. In that moment, all I could do was look at her and respond, "Well, aren't you cute?"

Oh, Brittany, sweet, sweet, innocent Brittany, I am so happy that you have embarked on this life goal of working with children. But holy cow, girlfriend, I nearly lost my ever-lovin' mind on you at Register Six that day.

Because what you didn't see was 10 minutes earlier, when two of my four-year-olds brought down an entire mannequin display in the lingerie department for fun. You also didn't witness them hide my car keys in the baking cabinet, causing a three-hour delay and garbage can search, and you most certainly didn't catch them coloring on our brand new kitchen table with markers.

There's no doubt in my mind that coming down to a child's level, speaking calmly, and discussing emotions are beneficial acts. But when you have multiple children, all usually needing something at the exact same time, the ability to turn into Dr. Phil while also paying at the register is not going to happen.

My point, dear Brittany, and anyone else who likes to give advice at Target, is unless you've walked in my shoes on my sticky floors covered in the yogurt the boys threw before we even left the house, don't offer any parenting tidbits.

You didn't witness my calming voice at 5:45 A.M. when they came bolting into my room. It became sterner by 10:00 A.M., when they climbed onto the hood of the car while I got things loaded. By noon, when they broke the blinds in the kitchen, I started to lose my cool. At 4:00 P.M., when you witnessed me yell at my kids, they had already tested me countless times and I was exhausted beyond belief.

The best thing anyone can do when they see a Hot Mess Express parent struggling to keep it together? Simple. Hold a door open, stop a child from bolting down the aisle by blocking them, or just simply walk by and say, "You're doing a great job. Keep it up."

Whether you've got one child or 10, special needs or strong-willed, each of our experiences is uniquely ours. And whether you're putting your toddler in a time-out in the frozen food section or yelling at him in the parking lot to get in the car, more power to you. So much of parenting is survival, and the best thing we can do to support one another on this crazy journey is be cheer-leaders, because let's face it: We all doubt ourselves enough already, and there's no universal instruction book for how to manage it all.

So to all the Brittanys of the world, keep rocking those classes. If you really want to help me out the next time you see my circus of a life in the checkout line, hand my kids a lollipop, tell them a joke, and call it a day. Because the last thing a mom deep in the trenches of survival needs to hear is what she "should" be doing. Instead of discipline, maybe give advice on which wine to pair with the next tantrum.

~

Learning to Ignore Judgment

This has been one of the hardest skills for me to learn, as I've always been far too concerned with what people think of me. Throw children in the mix, and that judgment is now completely out of your hands. You can make every effort possible to look put-together and have well-behaved children. But at the end of the day, if one of them feels like karate chopping a mannequin's arm off, you're out of luck with looking perfect.

Ignoring others' judgment is crucial to motherhood and keeping your sanity, because no matter where you are, people will judge you. From airplanes to the grocery store, there's always going to be someone giving you a side-eye or making a comment that makes you crumble inside.

For me, personally, the key is to constantly remind myself that my children are just that: kids. They are little and shouldn't be expected to be perfect all the time. I also remind myself that those judging are not perfect either, and at the end of the day, their opinion truly doesn't matter. One way to cope is to find a kind yet witty comeback like, "Oh, bless your heart." You can also just be blunt and respond, "So sorry.

They're children. They haven't learned to be perfect all the time yet."

When these moments arise—and they will—remind yourself that for every judging person, there are 10 who want to support and help you. Don't let the one who woke up on the wrong side of the bed get in your head.

14

LEARNING TO TAKE NOTHING FOR GRANTED

AT THE END OF THE DAY, IT'S ALL REALLY SMALL STUFF

On one cold, winter afternoon in 2016, I became enraged at one of my kids for chucking a wooden truck down the basement stairs and busting yet another hole in the wall.

"Seriously! What the heck is wrong with you?!" I screamed in anger.

My blood was boiling for the millionth time that day.

If one child wasn't shredding a box of muffin mix and sprinkling it all over the kitchen, his brother was shoving wooden puzzle pieces into the heater vents or flushing Crayons down the toilet. One brother punched another, resulting in a busted nose that bled all over our cream-colored carpet while I was in the middle of a shower. My husband was traveling for work, and my oldest had a school project due the next day that required craft paint and glitter, two of my arch nemeses, as I believe glitter is the herpes of crafting. I was at a breaking point and felt overwhelmed by the constant chaos around me, as if I was trying to clean up a wreckage site while an active tornado spun around me each and every day.

I once wore a pedometer for a week, curious to see my steps as I chased around four boys, cleaning up mess after mess after mess. I was averaging 18,000 steps a day without even going to the gym. That's a lot of milk spills and pee-stained bathrooms to clean daily.

Just as I finished yelling about the newest destruction, I got a phone call from my mother-in-law, who shared that a family friend's son had just been diagnosed with stage four cancer. He was only four years old—a mere 12 months older than my triplets, on whom I was currently losing my mind. He had been experiencing some stomach pain and then started having difficulty going to the bathroom. Doctors had originally thought maybe a hernia was causing the issues, but once the scans were complete, they got the devastating news that he had a mass in his abdomen.

In that single moment, time froze.

I developed a pit in my stomach, my heart aching for a family who had an uncertain, emotional roller coaster ahead. I felt their pain in a very raw way, unable to comprehend what getting news like that would feel like or how they would go forward. When you receive that kind of news, how do you even brush your teeth, put on your clothes, and make a meal, let alone go out in public and carry on conversations with others?

I can't even imagine going to a playdate or chatting with a mom at pick-up about mundane problems like tattling or toddler destruction while dealing with a sick child. Everything that once bothered me, would become obsolete.

As the TV blared Nick Jr. and the oven timer buzzed for dinner, I sat on the floor cleaning up muffin mix, staring at my room full of rambunctious, healthy boys, and thanked God.

Not a day went by that following year that I didn't think about that family, and in exchange, realize all the things I stressed and worried about were ridiculous.

It was all small, insignificant stuff.

The five pounds I gained over the holidays, meant nothing. My bone structure alone prevents me from ever being the skinniest girl in a room, so seriously, who cares? I gained those pounds making memories with my kids and enjoying the season with the ones I love. A dent in my car, created by an anonymous child slamming their scooter into the side to "see what would happen," is really not that big of a deal. We have transportation.

Our bathroom will continue to smell like a urinal for the next several years, no matter how much I scrub with Clorox, and that's OK. We have a roof over our heads. Each day I will continue to step on a LEGO or Hot Wheel and lose my mind. It's all good, because my little boys are healthy enough to play with their toys. And every blue moon, when our day unravels into a heap of mess, we'll have McDonald's drive-thru for dinner, and we'll all live to tell about it.

I'll never understand why life requires such dire situations to remind us all what's truly important. We go about our days allowing the silliest of things to get us down.

Go get the ice cream cone with your kids. Leave the laundry and jump in on a game of tag in the front yard. These moments are fleeting and never guaranteed beyond the present.

Learning to Take Nothing for Granted

On any given day in motherhood, it's very easy to lose sight of the preciousness that's right before you. One could even argue it's natural to get caught up in the ho hum of everyday life and focus on trivial things versus the gifts we've been given from God. At the end of the day, my family means more to me than any event I'm supposed to attend or dress I should fit into. My time spent with them is more valuable than anything else on earth, yet it's easy to get caught up in the trials and tribulations of life and lose focus. It isn't until something stops you in your tracks that you take a moment to step back and realize how blessed you are.

We shouldn't need a tragedy to put things into prospective. Practicing daily gratitude can consistently bring the things that truly matter to the forefront of your mind.

If you're religious, it may be a prayer in the morning, thanking God for the blessings in your life. Or it might be keeping a nightly journal of things for which you're grateful. As mothers, we may still lose our minds when the TV blares cartoons and someone puts a box of Crayons in the microwave, but these small daily acts remind us that as long as our people are OK, our world is great today.

15

LEARNING TO SIMPLIFY

THEY ARE TWO; THEY WON'T REMEMBER THE MAGIC
KINGDOM

When my oldest was turning two, I planned an epic birthday party for him. It was a "Balloon-a-Palooza." We blew up hundreds of balloons, stringing them with fishing line and hanging them throughout every room to make them look as if they were floating on the ceiling. The entire house was decked out in primary colors from top to bottom. It was a visual delight. We hired someone to paint faces, and I put together goodie bags filled with bubble wands, sidewalk chalk, and other colorful things. My mom baked a rainbow-layered cake from scratch that was bigger than my son. She blew up so many balloons her lips swelled up like Lisa Rinna's from a latex reaction. God bless mamas, right?

It took me an entire week to set up for the party. The house looked perfect. My Type A self would not overlook a single detail. Even our clothes coordinated with the party colors. It looked like a darn curated Pinterest event, and it was awesome.

And my son was miserable and cried through the entire thing.

No one—not his grandparents, nor his friends from school, nor neighbors he loved—could get him to smile that day. He was overstimulated, overwhelmed, and miserable.

We have pictures of him crying as a room full of people sing "Happy Birthday." The scene is such an oxymoron. A precious little boy, in the midst of a well-planned, over-the-top party, is just completely miserable. It still makes me sad to look at the photos. He hated every minute of the party, and it was a major wake-up call for me about what truly matters when our kids are little.

When I look back now—and really, even weeks later —I realize that I intended for my son to have a fun party, but ultimately it was more for me. I assumed he would enjoy this elaborate shindig I had planned, because that's what I would have loved as a kid. But at that time in his life, it wasn't his jam. He would have been completely thrilled with pancakes with Mom and Dad and a trip to the toy store. He didn't need the pomp and circumstance of turning 24 months. He just wanted his people, which at the time included my husband and me. That and a cupcake were all he truly needed.

Keep this is mind, young moms, because we all get caught up in the game. We all watch what our friends do or what we see on Pinterest or any other social media platform and we think, *Well, shoot, my kid needs that level of fabulousness too.*

But in reality, they don't. They need you and a cupcake. That is seriously it. And oh, by the way, they're two; they won't remember a single moment of this.

The following year, we went to a train-themed restaurant for dinner with two of his little playmates. I made him a cake with Thomas the Train riding on KitKat track ties, and he acted as if he'd won the lottery. His birthday was finally about him and what he truly wanted.

Having children gives us so many opportunities to make fun, new memories. Maybe you're like me and you had a magical mom who made every holiday a dreamy experience. Or maybe you had a crummy childhood, and because of that, you work overtime to make sure your child has the absolute best.

Whether you had it all or are making up for lost

experiences, rest assured your child won't remember Disney on Ice at 18 months old, so that $300 you just spent on tickets, light-up wands, and popcorn has just gone down the drain. You may remember it, and if your toddler is well behaved and it's a positive experience, then awesome! New memories made for you, the adult! But if you have a gaggle of children like I do, and every activity you attend costs a million dollars, lower your expectations and hold off before attempting the major ones. They won't remember or appreciate them, and you'll spend a fortune and lose your mind in the moment trying to corral your kids.

Over time, I've learned the hard way that lowering expectations is the only way to survive the early years.

We've spent thousands of dollars attempting events with our kids only to realize that two of the four hate it and make things miserable for everyone, or they're too young to enjoy it, leaving me praying just to get through it with our sanity intact.

At the end of the day, if you're choosing to spend the money on a trip to Disney World or LEGO Land before your kids are even out of training pants, understand that the trip is really for you, not them. And if you're cool with that, and have always wanted to spin around in some teacups at 33 years old, well, dreams come true. But if I can teach you anything from wrangling two-year-old triplets through a performance of *A Christmas Carol*, it's this: Sometimes the very things you think you're doing for your kids are really about you. I know you have it in your mind that you need to make these special memories with these little precious people, but in reality, they won't remember a single second of it. So, if an experience is for your memory bank, go forth! But if you're suffering through it in hopes that your children will create some lifelong memory, girl, turn in your chips. They will get just as much joy from a cup lid and the McDonald's Play Place as they will from Six Flags.

$\sim$

Learning to Simplify

I would be the biggest hypocrite on earth if I sat here and said I never indulged my kids. Nothing makes me happier than doing something with them that they love, like going to see a movie they're excited about or surprising them with pajamas with their favorite characters on them.

Doing things that bring you and your child equal joy is an awesome part of the parenting experience. The main lesson I learned from my son's second birthday party is that it's best for me to approach experiences with a checks and balances approach. I can get very excited about going to an event or having a certain family outing, but I've got to stop myself and weigh the pros and cons. Will all four of them have fun? Is it worth the money? Is it too much? Should we divide and conquer?

I think the key in learning to simplify is to recognize whether what you're doing with your child is for them or for you. You don't need to keep up with the Joneses; you just need to create happiness within your own family, however that may look.

16

LEARNING TO ACCEPT THE EBBS AND FLOWS

DEEP IN THE TRENCHES OF MOMHOOD

I remember the first time I felt like I was truly at war in my own home, against a tiny army I created myself.

At the time, my husband traveled for work four days a week, so I managed the chaos single-handedly Monday through Thursday. The triplets had just turned three and were running amok. On this particular morning, they plunged into the bathtub and turned on the faucet 10 minutes after I'd dressed them for the day. They were drenched from head to toe, shoes and all. They also slipped a toy into the oven, so when I preheated it to make lunch, a plastic smell filled the air and the toy melted into a pile of toxic goo. After they'd eaten, we all retreated to my bedroom, and I sneaked into the bathroom to soak my shirt in a sink full of hot water because they'd secretly colored on me with markers during lunch.

That's when I heard a crash.

I emerged from the master bathroom to discover that my children had rocked my dresser back and forth vigorously, causing the TV on top of it to tumble down. Scared to death someone had been hurt, I was already in a panic before realizing we were going to be late to pick up my oldest from kindergarten. We jumped in the car in a hurry, and the triplets screamed at each other while I navigated the pickup line at school. A few moms tried to stop and chat at my window, but I had to decline to participate in conversation due to the volume of toddler screams reverberating from the back seat. (Also, I really didn't want them peeking in to say hello to the boys anyway, because the level of disgust in my vehicle embarrassed me.) When my oldest got in the car he was ranting about something that happened on the playground at recess, and the noise got louder. Then they all proceeded to yell at each other for interrupting. My eye started twitching. I took some deep breaths and shoved some Skinny Pop in my mouth, attempting not to lose it.

Once we arrived back home, I walked in the door and instantly saw it: the water.

Water was pouring through the ceiling of our dining room. In the midst of my panic about the TV fiasco and running late, I had forgotten to shut off the sink, flooding the bathroom and causing about $1,000 of drywall damage. I flew up the stairs, losing my ever-loving-mind, while my children looked on, shocked by my crazy state.

This is what being in the trenches of momhood feels like.

Your head is constantly on a swivel, waiting for the next bomb to drop, and you're mentally inundated with war plans and strategy. There are so many moving parts, and your tiny army has you surrounded. In a matter of 30 minutes my children have drenched me with hoses in the garden department at Walmart, then turned around and dumped an entire Costco-sized container of cheese balls all over the car. They hang their heads climbing into the car as I yell at them, all while stomping on the cheeseballs and drilling them into my car's carpeting. I wish I was making this up. My poor car is the true hero of this entire book—no joke.

The baby and toddler years of parenting feel like being at war. There's uncertainty around every corner, and you wake up each morning, often still reeling from an attack the day before, and head right back into the fight. Sometimes you have victories, like not losing anyone at the park or a surprisingly pleasant meal out.

And a lot of the time you accept defeat, retreating back to the trench to seek solace.

One particular week, I had to wave the white flag to the army and the universe. On a Tuesday afternoon I received a call from school that one of the triplets wasn't feeling well. They were two years old at the time and attending a little Montessori school. I went to pick up the ill triplet, and we cruised over to a walk-in clinic to get checked out, as we didn't have time to make it to the pediatrician before needing to return to grab everyone else at dismissal. The doctor on duty looked him over and diagnosed him with Hand-Foot-Mouth virus, which was making him miserable. My mind raced with worry about all four catching it, because don't fool yourselves, people: nine times out of 10, if an illness comes through your doors, the entire house is getting it.

Before she finished examining him, the doctor quickly glanced at his light blond hair and turned to me with a look on her face that could only mean one thing. On top of the virus that would now make him scream for 48 hours straight, he also had lice.

Yes, lice.

To me, "lice" is one of the most disgusting words in the English dictionary. It's up there with "moist" and "curdled." The idea of it creeps me out beyond belief, and now it, too, was coming home to my house. On that drive home, I felt as though I was truly going into battle, and I wasn't sure I was going to emerge the victor or even remain standing at the end of it all. Even now, I think back to that week as one of the toughest in my parenting history.

After I grabbed the other three boys from school, I immediately raced them all into the bathroom for medicated shampoo treatments and buzz cuts. I treated my own hair as well, as just the thought of these parasites in my home made me start to itch all over. We had to strip all bedding, wash it in hot water, and then place it in big black trash bags outside for the next 48 hours. On top of that, I called in carpet cleaners to steam the furniture, carpets, and beds. While all of this was going on, the other two triplets began showing signs of Hand-Foot-Mouth virus, so the level of miserable in our house was at a 12. Because we now had no bedding, we huddled up with sleeping bags for two nights, and my phone call that evening with my husband went a little something like this.

Me: "Oh, hey Mark, how's everything going in Omaha?"

Mark: "Brutal day. The hotel had my reservation wrong and I ended up in a terrible room. I just finished up at the gym and still have a bunch of work to get done tonight, but I'm going to order some room service first. How's everything there?"

Me: "Well, a portal to hell has opened and sucked us all in."

On days like this one, when everything completely falls apart, I've learned to let go of my inner control freak, because I truly have no other choice. I can try to prevent my other kids from getting sick by dousing them in sanitizer and rubbing oils all over them, but all that will be undone when the infected child walks over and coughs right in their face. And that will happen, every single time. When a day like this happens, you just batten down the hatches, load up on supplies, and weather the storm until it passes. One Thanksgiving, when the triplets were barely one, we discovered that patient zero had attended the gathering. From that night on, every family member who was present came down with an awful stomach bug that lasted for days. It took down all four of my boys, as well as my husband and me. We inevitably had to call my mother-in-law and say, "We know you're going to catch this, and we're sorry, but you need to come into the war zone. We can't physically care for the boys right now because we are so sick."

Here's the thing with the trenches: to some degree, you will always be in them. There will always be some level of chaos. Your day might fall apart because of sports scheduling conflicts instead of toddler destruction, but there will always be a level of crazy. One day you'll have a teenager who won't emote or share what's going on in their head, versus your now toddler who expresses everything, including when they need to poo.

That said, the anxiety-provoking anarchy levels that the baby and toddler years bring do pass and become manageable. Kids' ability to reason develops. They stop crying because you gave them the wrong color socks. They begin eating meals without massive food fights that stain the walls with spaghetti sauce. Well, we're still working on that one, but you catch my drift.

Slowly but surely, the insanity levels will calm and you will be able to rise up from the trenches and enjoy the experience without its paired chaos. And when you climb out of the foxhole, hopefully you will be able to finally look back and laugh at the disgusting "what the hell?!" moments you've experienced. As I've moved through the years of my children making poop art on their nursery walls and throwing food from our fridge all over our back patio to "feed the ants," I've kept chanting to myself, *I will look back one day and laugh. I will look back one day and laugh.*

And you know what? We do laugh now. We think back to the insanity of it all, mostly the parts our brains haven't blocked out to protect us, and we laugh.

Learning to Accept the Ebbs and Flows

For all my dear, precious readers who are currently in the trenches, I swear on all that is holy, you seriously will look back one day and laugh.

It's hard to envision that now, but you will—I promise with my whole heart.

And as you're laughing about the diaper disasters of the past, you'll find yourself shaking your head all over again at a new set of issues. Bigger kids mean bigger problems. When they're little you're simply trying to keep them alive and stop them from eating their own poop. But as they grow and develop their own little personalities and attitudes, an entirely new circus show begins.

Looking back and laughing at the ebbs and flows of the toddler years is what gets me through my new normal of homework meltdowns, lying, and all the other not-so-fun stuff that comes with older kids.

There are tough days, and there are really good days. It's all part of the journey. Each time I call my mom on a good day, she responds with, "Soak this up. Go celebrate. You need to cherish the good ones."

17

LEARNING TO SURVIVE THE TOUGH DAYS

THE PRESSURE COOKER EFFECT

S ometimes, during dinners at my house, I feel like I am one dropped glass of milk away from a mental breakdown. It's typically what spurs the nightly glass of wine, or my need to sit in a quiet space like the bathroom for 20 minutes so I don't go all Jerry Springer guest on my kids.

When I explain to my husband what my anxiety feels

like, I tell him it's like being a human pressure cooker. The spilled cup of milk that floods the kitchen table and soaks everyone's chicken nuggets is the last bit of steam that makes the lid pop off. But the pressure has been building all day.

It begins in the morning, when we rush out the door and my boys fight over seats in the car. This typically results in them sitting on top of one another, body slamming each other into the windows, and inevitably breaking some piece of plastic off of my car. Like most kids, they ask me about our plans for the day, proceed to forget said plans, and ask again 30 seconds later like Dory from *Finding Nemo*. When a child does this, it is sweet and endearing. But when four children do it at the same time while you're trying to back out of the garage and not side swipe the fence in the process, it grates at your nerves.

Once we arrive at School Drop-off Number One, it becomes clear that while I remembered the ice skates and Cub Scouts uniform for later that evening, I neglected to grab the lunches on the way out the door.

"Mom, seriously? How could you forget the lunches? We're going to starve," says one child who is no longer in the running for my favorite.

During School Drop-off Number Two, in which I have to shuffle three children with three each of backpacks, nap mats, folders, letter bags, and lunches to three different classrooms, I inevitably lose my car keys somewhere in the building. This is so common it's become a running joke among the teachers. It's probably time for me to invest in a fanny pack, especially since they're back in style now.

On non-school days, things are even worse. Running from activity to activity and making sure we have everything we need, is a big task. But adding in the child who is now in full-blown hysterics because he can't find LEGO Luke Skywalker's light saber, ratchets up my stress level. While he's flipping out about a one-inch piece of plastic, another is shouting, "Why won't you do art with me? You never do anything with me."

Wow, child, thanks for reminding me that there aren't enough hours in the day to be a superhuman mom to four kids. Thanks for affirming for me I'm not doing a good enough job. Man, the things your kids say in their moments of anger can really sting.

My anxiety compounds even more as we head home from school and the low tire pressure light comes on. I won't have time to stop and have it checked because my oldest has soccer skills practice and one of my triplets must be home in time for his allergy medication. When we come home and pull into the garage, we spot a huge trash mess all over the driveway, because I didn't properly put the lid on the can when we left early that morning and some neighborhood critter had a field day.

One day after school drop-offs, I came home, let out a huge relaxing sigh, and headed for the shower. As I pulled the black running headband off my head, I noticed a dark blue line of ink across my bleached blonde hair. Some child had taken a pen and colored the headband, and now I would spend the remainder of the day with a racing stripe.

As the boys' arguing continues through dinner, I walk to the table, find half their vegetables on the floor, and lose it. I'm out of patience, and I yell, scream, and lose my shizz—and then immediately feel guilty about it.

Yelling contributes to major mom guilt, because the minute you do it and you look at their sweet little faces, you feel bad you did it. But at the same time, a human can only be pushed so far before smoke comes out of their ears.

Some nights my husband comes home to find me wrangling our four children into pajamas and battling about teeth brushing. He takes one look at the crazy in my eyes and immediately takes over, for everyone's safety. Adding to the steam in the pressure cooker are all the things that I didn't accomplish that day, which are still waiting for me once my kids go to sleep: packing four lunches for the next day, cleaning up after dinner, the six loads of laundry waiting to be folded, and the pool of urine that surrounds each potty, needing to be wiped.

Motherhood is downright exhausting. There's no other way to put it. And being Type A, I'm not really able to collapse onto the couch at the end of the day to relax until the kitchen has been cleaned and toys have been put away. While my husband doesn't even notice the mess, it irks me beyond belief.

I wish I could say that the pressure cooker effect has gotten better, but it's still a daily struggle and something I work to improve every day. There are always going to be days when those four boys get the best of me and I yell. I'm a yeller, who must shout to be heard often, whether to discipline or just to gather their attention to explain something. Trying to get my boys to pay attention to me is like trying to talk to a friend at a heavy metal concert. They see my lips moving, but the sheer volume of noise and chaos in our home prevents them from comprehending what I'm saying.

What helps me manage how my yelling affects my kids, is a simple shift in how I handle the lid blowing off the cooker. In moments when I find myself shouting and my boys looking shocked as though they're waiting for me to turn into Ursula from *The Little Mermaid*, I find a way to turn the yelling into something humorous. I begin yelling in a funny voice, or start chasing them around the house to "smack their booties" in a silly way. Their expressions change from scared to cracking up, and it's a good reality check to remind me that they are little and don't know any better.

They are tiny little people still trying to learn and figure it all out, and if I can keep that in mind, I can also attempt to keep the pressure cooker at a simmer.

～

Learning to Survive the Tough Days

Unless you're trained by the military to handle interrogation, I think most humans have a breaking point when it comes to stress. And for those who are home all day long with little ticking time bombs, you're bound to experience days when your pressure cooker lid blows off. Just a few days into a family vacation, my husband's eye starts twitching from the noise of being with our kids all day long.

Finding ways to approach the situation with humor can definitely change the mood in the room, and if that doesn't work, grab some chocolate, your phone, a glass of wine or whatever your vice is, and find a nice dark closet to take refuge in for a few moments.

18

LEARNING TO BE VULNERABLE

THE NIGHTLY POUR

I t's 7:00 P.M. on a Tuesday, and it's time for a reward, stress break, and pat on the back for surviving yet another day of mothering.

You see, my alarm went off at 5:00 A.M. From that moment on, I dressed and fed four kids; completed a school drop-off; went to speech therapy and gymnastics class; hit the gym; battled Costco with three littles in tow; took a trip to the veterinarian's office; suffered through four meltdowns, homework struggles, and karate class;

and cooked dinner, which included placing green veggies on their plates and enduring only one food fight. I also answered around 250 questions about zombies, space shuttles, gravity, the sun, and farts. That all took place in between two loads of laundry, a phone call with the power company, and sewing on a Cub Scout badge.

To some, this may seem insane, but this is my normal every day. And on a good day, we arrive at all of these activities and appointments on time. On a bad day, some child biffs it in the parking lot, requiring an additional visit to urgent care, or I get a phone call from school that someone is throwing up. Then all hell breaks loose because there's a chink in the chain.

Chinks in the chain are problematic for types like me. My household runs like a well-greased machine, so if one cog in the wheel busts, the entire conveyer belt overloads and Mama loses her mind.

Every single day of my life is a marathon, and with nine years of motherhood under my belt, including six with triplets, the need to reward myself for surviving another 24 hours had become standard practice.

Seven o'clock in the evening, for me, means most days my major mom duties are coming to an end and it's time to treat myself with a glass of Pinot Noir and alleviate the stress. It's almost as if my entire body inhales and exhales as I pop the cork. My shoulders relax, and my eye stops twitching. I've had virtual "cheers" via Face-Time with friends throughout the country doing the exact same thing. We support one another through the daily struggles. We've even had matching wine glasses engraved with our "Mom Gang" slogans. We laugh over drinking memes that ring so true to reality. We use a glass of wine to celebrate the highs and to commiserate the lows. And because of that, my nightly eight ounces had become a habit—one I set out to break and failed at doing so a million times until now.

As I approached my late 30s, the desire to kick the habit became even more important to me, as studies have shown a link between alcohol consumption and cancer. I'd never seen my nightly pour of vino as problematic because I indulged in only a single glass and, well, antioxidants.

But I didn't like my habit. I didn't like relying on something for stress, and I needed to find a way out of the cycle I had swirled into while sniffing sweet notes and observing tannins. (You take one trip to Napa and you're suddenly a wine connoisseur of sorts with the verbiage!)

I remember my husband's concern with my consumption when the triplets were two. I went to my doctor and explained my circumstances. His advice at the time was to keep drinking.

No,

you didn't misread that.

My doctor told me to decant that goodness.

"Based on your life, you have a stress-induced panic

disorder," he said. "I could put you on medication, but that won't help much because meds are temporary and your situation isn't going to get any easier for years."

Thanks for the reminder, Doc.

For the longest time, my friends and I died laughing over the fact that my doctor prescribed booze as my cure. Quite frankly, it wasn't very responsible of him. I mean, don't some people fudge the truth about their intake on doctors' forms? I could have been sipping dry martinis at noon while swerving my mom wagon around town for school pick-up for all he knew. It happens. I've witnessed a mom receive a midday field sobriety test in front of a church preschool before. It wasn't pretty.

Many young moms fall into the allure of drinking to solve their problems. Our generation is great at connecting and sharing our lives, and we've made drinking wine to get through it all part of the experience. Every single time I text a friend about something ridiculous that's happened or post a picture of outrageous things my kids have done, they immediately respond, "Crack open the wine, sister!" with a cute little emoji. Our culture accepts and celebrates wine as a motherhood cure-all—and sometimes it can be. But when it turned into every single night, for me it became too much.

When I decided last fall to finally reevaluate my relationship with wine, I sought out the help of Kelley Kitley, a nationally known psychotherapist in Chicago. For six weeks I abstained from alcohol and "faced the music," as they say. It was difficult but eye-opening.

I ended up interviewing Dr. Kitley for an article I was working on, and her answers were so compelling that I wanted to share them here for any other moms who may feel stuck in a nightly rut.

I don't ever remember my mom or my friends' moms drinking much when I was a kid, and most of my friends don't either. Is this mom/wine relationship new, or has it grown?

KITLEY: It has always gone on; it just wasn't talked about back in the day. Today, with social media, women have more platforms to share with one another, and in a way, it's normalized [drinking alcohol] to make people feel more comfortable with it. I've certainly seen alcohol use gone up as well. We're all a lot busier these days, trying to manage everything.

So if I have only one glass a night, how do I know if I have a problem?

KITLEY: Well, anything done repetitively can become problematic. You'll see more and more health detriment, and as we know, breast cancer rates have gone up, [which are] associated with alcohol use.

Is this an American problem or a middle- to upper-class problem?

KITLEY: No, this is a global problem. I believe China has the highest level of alcohol-related deaths among women. And while one mom in the U.S. may be reaching for wine, the one who can't afford that may be reaching for a 40. The problem reaches all demographics and races.

So what can I do to break my cycle?

KITLEY: They say it takes 21 days to truly break a habit. If the witching hour is when you typically pour a glass, you still need to reward yourself in some way during that time of day. You may also want to change the atmosphere. Instead of a glass of wine, pour a La Croix in a wine glass with cut up fresh fruit, and maybe turn on some music and dance with your kids. You need to still have something to look forward to.

Do I have to give up wine completely? What if I want to break the nightly routine but still be able to enjoy an occasional night out?

KITLEY: When we look at the big picture it's better to quit completely, but it's really hard. Our society is very social. It's important to be mindful of the habit and be aware of if it's sneaking back. With my patients I call it modification management. You wouldn't sit down and eat 10 big cookies in a row, so why would you allow yourself that many drinks? It's a work in progress.

What do you say to those who truly enjoy the stress relief of a glass?

KITLEY: It's difficult, because it's true: within 10 minutes of drinking a glass of wine, you do feel more relaxed and calmer. But over time with alcohol use, people can become more anxious and depressed. And women need to remember that we process alcohol much faster than men.

~

Learning to be Vulnerable

Vulnerability is one of the most difficult emotions for a Type A person. Exposing that things are not OK, that they're not as perfect as they appear from the outside, can be crippling.

One thing my husband has always said he loves most about me is my strength and ability to handle all that life throws at me. You can imagine the heavy feelings I had when having to accept that I needed help. I felt like a failure and a fraud. I'd walk past people in the store as they told me I was "Supermom" or "a saint." I'd smile and thank them, trying to look like I had it all together while simultaneously crumbling inside.

When I chose to seek out therapy, I didn't have to stop drinking wine, but I made the choice to, because if I was going to spend three months digging into my anxiety and triggers, I wanted to face the truth sober as can be.

While my wine consumption never got to a troublesome place, it masked emotion that I was shoving deep down and concealing with Napa varietals.

With motherhood come so many personal expectations, emotions brought up from the past, and demands from society. And with vulnerability comes authenticity. That moment you finally pull back the curtain and face what's paralyzing you from being your best? It's freeing.

Having gone through that therapy gave me a new perspective on life. Instead of striving to be "Perfect Mom," I work toward being "Authentic Mom." That experience gave me the courage to write this book, and I encourage anyone who feels overwhelmed to step out of their comfort zone and talk to someone. It may seem scary at first, but laying it all out there will lift so many feelings of guilt and inadequacy off of your shoulders.

19

LEARNING TO SLOW DOWN

YOU'RE GOING TO MISS THIS

I f you ever find yourself pondering over a cup of coffee or while zoning out in the car line when you will officially become an "old hen," the answer is when you tell a younger mother, "You're going to miss this, and it will pass in the blink of an eye."

It's a phrase my mother-in-law has told me throughout the entire raising-tiny-dictators phase, and while I know she's right and the statement is factual, it's difficult to appreciate when they're screaming and slinging poo-filled diapers at your head.

"The days are long, but the years are short," is another classic line from mothers of grown children to those of us in the trenches.

These statements come from wise women who have dealt with the poo, the colic, and the grocery store melt-downs—and they're right. One day, your kids go off to kindergarten, and in the blink of an eye, they're gradu-ating high school and you're wondering where it all went. The hard part is the five years leading up to said kindergarten when you are on a legitimate battleground of keeping tiny humans alive while maintaining some shred of sanity.

"You're gonna miss this," is a truthful statement that also riddles moms with so much guilt. Like many, I went through this guilt cycle every single day when my boys were toddlers.

It would start around afternoon. I'd be up to my elbows in literal poop. No joke—there were smears on the walls that smelled like a monkey's cage. I'd discover that someone tossed a diaper into the washer during the rinse cycle, resulting in a load of laundry covered in exploded, moisture-wicking gel material a la Pampers. An hour later, they'd wake up from their naps scream-ing, and one would head-butt me to the point of seeing stars. Moments later, I'd find a granola bar shoved in the DVD player and later discover that one had painted the bathroom tile with my nail polish. Everyone protested dinner; they flooded the floors during bath time; and seemingly every day, I'd forget that the next day was some kind of absurd dress-up day at my oldest's school, forcing us to pile in the car to run to the store for a last-minute costume.

Let me tell you, old hens, I'm surely not going to miss any of this! I'd think to myself while cleaning up the pig trough that was my kitchen table.

At the end of the poop-filled day, after a glass of wine and loads of silent "what the hell?" mental queries, I'd tuck them into bed. They would fight bedtime and I could hear them jump from bed to bed, throwing their bodies against the walls. I'll never forget sitting on my couch one night as they turned their bedroom into the Thunderdome and watching a framed photograph fall off of the wall and shatter because their brute force shook the house's framework.

I'd finally collapse on the couch with a bowl of popcorn and a trash reality show to escape my thoughts. As I attempted to watch the housewives duke it out, the sounds of screaming, complaining children at dinnertime echoed in my ears. I'd spend about an hour exhausted, feeling defeated and overwhelmed at the idea that I must get up in the morning, put on my big girl pants, and participate in this whole charade all over again.

As I finally headed up to bed, I'd stop by their rooms to make sure everyone had actually fallen asleep on a soft surface, and my heart would melt watching them dream peacefully. I'd immediately feel guilty for how much I'd yelled that day, and as I'd sit in the quiet looking at them, I'd find myself amazed by how much they'd grown and how they still told me they loved me every day despite my faults. Then again in the morning, they'd pop up one by one and sneak in my bedroom with big, glorious smiles, happy to greet the day and see their mama. After a night's sleep, I'd awake to find my spirit renewed and myself madly in love all over again with my little people.

"You're going to miss this" is an interesting concept, because in so many ways I don't now and am pretty sure I won't later on.

I don't miss the screaming, the excrement, the feeling like I don't have enough to give. I won't miss feeling like I'm failing my kids by losing my temper, even though they rarely even give it two seconds thought.

What I will miss is the simplicity of making them happy.

Someone hurt their feelings at school? A Dum-Dum or a trip for ice cream fixes it instantly.

One of them falls climbing a tree and scrapes their knee? A Spiderman Band-Aid and a big hug and kiss instantly heals the wound.

From the ages of 0–5 years old, kids are hard beyond words, but they are transparent and uncomplicated. They aren't yet dealing with playground politics, bullies, self-doubt, or challenges of academics and social norms.

Life is fleeting, and it speeds up the older we get. To those moms who struggle with a daily cycle of guilt, my advice is to live in the really good moments and celebrate them deeply.

Parenting comes with a lot of crap (pun intended), but it also comes with amazing little moments that happen now and again. After a few tiring weeks, you may experience a day when your child who struggles in school is selected as Student of the Month. Knowing how difficult school is for that child, you internalize their joy—because, as we all know, every happiness and heartache our children feel, we mothers feel 10 times more. Soak up that phone call from the headmaster; soak up that entire day. Forget your new diet trend and go for ice cream right after you pick up your kiddo from school. In fact, opt for two scoops or add sprinkles and revel in your child's happiness.

We don't know what tomorrow brings. It might be an ice cream sundae; it might be a shit show. The more we live in the present, the more we truly absorb in the heart.

~

Learning to Slow Down

You know those signs that read, "My floors are sticky and my sink is filled with dishes because my children are making memories"?

I can't stand that sign, because it gives the impression that to make memories you must let everything else go to hell. That's simply not true. So much of slowing down has nothing to do with quantity and more with quality.

When I ask my boys about some of their favorite memories from when they were tiny, they never remember the days I sat on the ground all afternoon playing trains. They remember little snippets, moments that didn't last long but delved deep in love and excitement. For example, they delight in our after-dinner dance parties, during which someone chooses a song and we have a dance-off. These only take five minutes of our day, but the memory of jamming out together every evening will likely stick with them as they grow.

Learning to slow down is more about training your mom brain to shut off for a bit while enjoying the moment with your kids. As you're trick-or-treating, holding your child's precious little hand, soak it up. Smell the crisp air, feel their adorable little grasp in your hand. Take a photo in your memory. Stop allowing cluttered thoughts to steal these little moments. One day when you're old and gray, you'll remember the special days when you were completely present, and you'll never regret slowing down to enjoy the moment.

20

LEARNING SELF-CARE

ALL YOU NEED IS POPCORN AND OPRAH

My mother-in-law once told me a story of a mom who was at a breaking point and needed a few moments to herself. It was the 1950s, and she was raising eight kids on the South Side of Chicago in a small bungalow home. One of her boys was acting particularly unruly, and in a moment of motherhood desperation, she tied him to the radiator to walk away and find a moment of silence.

No one batted an eye at these parenting tactics back then, but in today's world, it's practically considered child endangerment to take a shower while your kids are awake, and heaven forbid you answer a few emails instead of playing dress-up for 30 minutes.

Somewhere over the last 60 years, we moms have lost our way. We no longer carve out a few moments of sanity each day when we need them most. We've become programmed to think that every waking minute we're with our children should be about enrichment and togetherness. But for many, especially those with several kids, that's just not practical without losing your ever-loving mind.

How did society go from one extreme to another? Has there ever been a time in history when we weren't as extreme as tying children to appliances yet we didn't feel guilt for taking breaks from tiny humans who demand milk and Goldfish?

The answer is yes, and that timeframe is one of my favorite decades of all: the '90s.

When I was a kid, circa 1992, I used to go to after-school playdates at my friend Julie's house. She was one of five girls, and her mom was a teacher just like mine.

From 4:00–5:00 P.M., no one was allowed in the TV room except Julie's mom. For one hour a day, she enjoyed a Diet Coke, microwaved popcorn, and *The Oprah Winfrey Show*. Unless someone was dying and needed to go to the ER, you didn't dare step foot in that room. That was the rule, and everyone abided by it. Any burning questions or requests could wait.

That one hour of solitude was a necessity in her life, providing quiet and a chance to replenish her patience after teaching all day.

Back then, expecting your kids to entertain themselves for an hour was completely normal. Our moms didn't dote on us every waking second of the day. They were there for us when we needed them and loved us unconditionally, but also let us learn independence.

And guess what? We kids were totally fine during that 60 minutes of *Oprah*. We didn't grow up seeking therapy for abandonment issues because our mothers needed a break. And now that we're mothers, we completely understand why they did what they did.

I've often reminded myself of these life lessons from the '90s, because my four boys try to guilt me out of my own Zen daily. The concept is simple. The craft project can wait. Your kids won't starve from a lack of snacks in one hour. Find your *Oprah* and popcorn and remind yourself: the kids will survive 60 minutes of self-sufficiency and go on to lead normal, happy lives. You'll be happier too.

~

Learning Self-Care

We can learn so much from the generations before us.

We can learn from their mistakes and successes with the goal of bettering ourselves and continuing to evolve as moms. For reasons unknown, we lost our way with regard to caring for ourselves and keeping our sanity, which are important for both our own happiness and our children's.

I personally feel technology plays a role in this feeling among moms that we can't leave our child's side for even a moment to catch our breath. When my mom raised me, she did what she thought was best and used her judgment. Nowadays, we moms are on social media, bombarded with articles about what's best and how we should do things—and those who choose to do things their own way often feel unrealistic judgment or mom shame.

Here's the deal: you deserve an hour of calm, and you'll be a better mom for it. Also, your entire life's work doesn't need to be curated by what you learn online. God gave you these babes to raise the way you see fit. The happiness and calm you'll find by carving out time for self-care will inevitably trickle down to your kids.

21

LEARNING TO KEEP YOUR IDENTITY

YOU'RE MORE THAN JUST A MOM

F amous Author Judy Blume graduated college in 1960, already married and pregnant with her first child. She hung her diploma over her washing machine.

When I first heard this from a friend, it hit me like a ton of bricks. While I didn't get married and start a family right out of college, I didn't wait around long either. I had always wanted a family, and I was torn on whether to stay home with my kids. I'd planned to return to work as the associate editor at the newspaper I'd been working for up until I delivered my first son, but as my maternity leave came to an end, my hormones —and my pay grade—prevented that from happening. Like many women, my entire paycheck would have been devoted to child care, and my husband and I were fortunate enough to be in a position where I could stay home. I made the decision to leave my job, but within the following year, I realized it wasn't the right decision for me.

The Type A in me was driven, and while my children are my world, I grew bored with the mundane parts of being at home. Sure, every day held adorable moments that I loved. I enjoyed snuggling in bed and watching cartoons each morning while Baby John drank his sippy cup of milk and I savored my first delicious cup of coffee. I loved meeting up with friends at the park or pool for a playdate and the flexibility of being able to travel to see family whenever we wanted. I cherished these little moments, but that's exactly what they were: tiny fragments of very long days. The special little moments comprised about 10 percent of the day; the other 90 percent consisted of meltdowns, laundry, dishes, vacuuming up Cheerios, changing yet another milk-stained onesie, and a lot of John and me just staring at each other. Being a stay-at-home mom also meant I became my husband's personal assistant, picking up dry cleaning and prescriptions, getting his oil changed, and more—because, you know, I'm home, so naturally all these responsibilities should fall on me, right? Society tells us so.

I'm fortunate to have some pretty amazing friends in my life, some of whom are partners in law and private wealth management firms, doctors, big-time realtors, and all-around boss babes. We've spent many a wine night throughout the years discussing how the grass is always greener. The stay-at-home moms wish they had a reason to get up and leave the house each day and use their brains for more than taxi services and sandwich making. And the full-time working moms wish they had less time at the office and more at home, constantly carrying the guilt that they're missing everything.

To me, the ideal situation would be working part-time when your kids are young. You'd live the best of both worlds. But unfortunately, not many companies hire employees who only work from 10:00 A.M. to 2:00 P.M. And if they do, they don't usually pay well. It's one reason you see so many stay-at-home moms working side hustles like selling skin care or essential oils. They still have the time at home with their kids, but they also have something that's just theirs in which to invest themselves.

Another part of the struggle comes when your youngest goes off to kindergarten and suddenly your sole purpose of being at home vanishes. What now? Do you try to go back to work after five plus years out of the workforce? Do you delve into charity work or step up to the plate in PTA to fill your days?

My triplets begin kindergarten this year, which is one of the driving forces in my returning to the professional writing world. This decision has reinvigorated the sense of gumption and moxie I once had at 22, before marriage and kids. Having something of my own, something that makes me more than just Mark's wife or John, Tommy, Teddy, and Nate's mom, has calmed anxieties I never knew existed and made me excited about life. *My* life, which is separate from being "just a mom."

To any mom who's contemplating whether or not to stay home, my advice is to do what your heart tells you to do. It's a vague answer to a complex question, I know, but honestly, your intuition will tell you what's best for you and your family. If you do decide to stay home, always keep your pinky toe in the adult pool, and never lose sight of the girl you once were before the family chapter of your book began. Whether it's through blogging, volunteering, taking a class here or there, or something else, always have a purpose—in addition to your children—that gives you self-worth. When you attend a dinner party and someone says, "What is it that you do?" have an answer in your pocket that's more than "I'm a stay-at-home mom." Because even though staying at home with your children is a tough job and a highly commendable career choice, I can't tell you the amount of times conversations have abruptly ended when those words came out of my mouth. People assume all I have to contribute is kid talk. The minute I changed my response to "writer," the doors opened, and suddenly I morphed into a much more interesting person to talk to.

And if you're a working mama, feeling the guilt of being at the office all day or on business trips, rest assured, you're not missing much. Sure, you may not be able to make the random Tuesday morning playdate, but you'll also miss the massive fit when you serve the macaroni and cheese you made for lunch on the wrong color plate. You'll pee without someone staring at you, and you'll make phone calls without people screaming in the background. The quality of the moments you share far outweighs the amount of time that ticks by on the clock. Did you kiss your kids when they woke up and tell them how special they are? Did you hug them extra tight at bedtime and hear about the art project they worked on that day? Then you're essentially enjoying the same quality moments, minus the mess and noise. And most importantly, your children know they're loved. My mom worked while I was growing up, and I had the most wonderful upbringing with loads of great memories. I never once felt like I missed anything because she worked during the day.

After I learned about Judy Blume, I dug out my framed diploma. My husband's three degrees have always hung prestigiously in our home office, but mine had been shoved in a cabinet, mixed in with old tax forms and printer paper. Instead of hanging it above my washer and dryer, I chose to display mine in my closet.

Each morning as I get dressed, that degree reminds me I'm more than just a mom and my next chapter is just about to be written.

∾

Learning to Keep Your Identity

Until the end of time, the grass will always be greener in the world of motherhood.

Whether you're sitting in a high-powered office missing a field trip or on your hands and knees at home cleaning up the fourth mess of the day, you'll always doubt and question your motherhood journey. It's human nature.

Then one day, your kids will grow up and leave. And your role as their mom will shift to supporter, often from afar. How you handle that chapter in life is linked to what you're doing now to keep your identity. If being a mom is all you've known for 18 plus years, then what? What brings you joy now? What will fulfill you when no one relies on you anymore?

We women have the distinct honor of bringing these babies into the world and raising them well, but we also have so much more to offer. Never lose sight of that young woman who had passions and goals for her life prior to starting her family. She's in there and deserves her time as well.

22

LEARNING TO TRUST YOUR GUT

GOD WINKS

W hen my oldest son was three years old, he didn't speak much. I wasn't overly concerned at the time, because both his dad and great-uncle were late talkers, as was Albert Einstein, so he had that going for him.

As he grew, his speech was still delayed, so we started him in therapy three times a week in an attempt to catch him up. As anyone who has a child with delays knows, therapists, doctors, teachers, and outspoken relatives will all offer their opinions of your child, and many times they're wrong.

If I had a dollar for every time someone suggested the wrong diagnosis for my son, I'd buy a new handbag.

At a parent/teacher conference when John was four, a teacher told me she believed something was seriously wrong with him, something he wouldn't grow out of, something that would be a lifelong disability.

I broke down sobbing in the conference. My palms began to sweat, and my face flushed. Panic washed over my body. In an instant, my hopes for his future, for what he may become, were crushed.

From the day our kids are born, we, as moms, begin fantasizing about their future. When John was a baby, he used to smile when I'd recite Dr. Seuss, so I was convinced he'd be an author. He used to love flipping light switches. *Boom!*—he was going to be an electrician. He loved stacking blocks, so he must want to be an engineer, right? Our mommy minds travel as we dream. It's probably a side effect of sleep deprivation and intense love.

In that room, with that teacher, all my hopes for my child disappeared. They were replaced with all-consuming worry: *Will he be bullied? Will he ever live independently? Will he ever get to experience true love or fatherhood?* Each internal question brought more tears and punches to the gut.

These thoughts filled me with sadness, and I went home and bawled my eyes out for the remainder of the day. I sat there looking at my beautiful, blue-eyed boy, knowing in my heart there was no possible way this teacher was right. Her degrees and certificates couldn't possibly compare to my mama gut. As moms, we begin to feel crazy when someone suggests something about our kids that we know not to be true. Others may see us as in denial, and oftentimes, we begin to believe it and question ourselves.

The following morning, with eyes swollen from sadness and an achy heart, I went grocery shopping with my little guy. As we approached the register to pay, I noticed our checker had a severe speech impediment. He greeted us with the biggest smile and said, "Hi! How are you guys this morning?" I had to listen a little harder, like I do when speaking with someone with a thick accent, but I was able to carry on a great conversation with him. He was probably about 23 years old, tall with an athletic build, with blonde hair and blue eyes, just like my little man. He was smart, charismatic, and happy. He had a wonderful, jovial laugh. As I swiped my credit card, I felt my eyes well up once again, but this time because I felt a spiritual presence.

I felt a God wink—a special moment of coincidence that feels divine, almost like a prayer in your thoughts has been answered or that guidance is being given. To feel a God wink, you have to be present, and you have to look for it.

In that moment, God did not tell me, but *showed* me that the worries that churned in my stomach were absurd. He told me that my little boy would grow up to be a happy member of society, even if his speech issues never faded.

That grocer helping us that day was no accident. And along with giving me comfort, God's wink also reaffirmed for me to trust my gut where my children are concerned. It's something I continue to do today, and I am happy to say my son is well into elementary school and thriving.

God winks come in many forms. Whether it's just being in the right place at the right time or stumbling upon an old letter from childhood with encouragement when you need it most, if you keep your head up and your mind present, you will find the universe reassuring you along your path in life.

God also guides us through intuition. When we trust our mama gut—our heart versus our brain—we often make the wiser decision. We second-guess ourselves because we are taught to think things through, weigh pros and cons, research, and come to an educated conclusion. Being Type A, I can't even count the amount of times in my life I've made lists and diagrams in my attempt to make the best decisions for my future. But often, especially when it comes to matters of our children and family, our gut feeling is the correct one. We typically know our answer within seconds, but our brain and society tell us to stop, think things through, and seek the advice of professionals. That's the logical thing to do, right?

Trusting my gut and that innate feeling inside have continued to serve me well as my oldest son has grown. Back when he was three, he developed an irritating, stubborn rash, and after medication couldn't cure it, doctors urged us to consider a painful skin biopsy to test for a lifelong autoimmune disorder. It gave my husband and me pause. John was a toddler. A biopsy seemed like an aggressive approach when we had not yet considered alternative ideas and treatments. We asked for a few months to make a decision and in the meantime made dietary changes to alleviate inflammation in his system. Within a week, the rash completely disappeared. Had we not trusted our gut, we would have put our son through the pain of having his skin punched out and possibly encountered an inaccurate diagnosis.

So the next time you're given a suggestion about your child's welfare that doesn't feel right, don't ignore that nagging feeling. Instead, home into your intuition and trust that guidance from within.

Learning to Trust Your Gut

To quote the amazing Forrest Gump, "Life is like a box of chocolates; you never know what you're gonna get."

There isn't a more factual movie quote out there, espe-

cially when dealing with your kiddos. Every single day presents new highs, lows, challenges, concerns, and joys. Just when you think you've got it all figured out, God reminds you that this experience is not a sprint to the finish line, but a journey filled with uphill climbs, losing your way, finding it again, and embracing contentment through the chaos. It very much resembles Dr. Seuss's Oh, the Places You'll Go!, *celebrating the highs of adventure and new beginnings to wading through the strife and loneliness of those phases that feel off-kilter. That book is a favorite gift for new moms to read to their baby, as he or she begins a new journey in life. But it serves purpose and meaning for the mom as well, for her life will never be the same after she becomes a mother. She, too, is on a new adventure.*

In motherhood, whether you're encountering the highest of highs or the lowest of lows, nothing will guide you more than your own intuition.

Nothing.

Use reason when it fits, prayer when it matters most, and always trust that voice from within. It's there for a reason.

23

LEARNING TO EMBRACE IT ALL

THIS IS THE HAND YOU USED TO HOLD

There is no expensive handbag, fancy perfume, or other gift I love more than the homemade art projects my kids bring home from school for Mother's Day.

I'm not talking about the daily pieces that come

covered in glitter glue and pompoms. The majority of those fly into the recycle bin, with the exception of a few special creations.

If you want to see me ugly cry, watch me fall into a puddle when they bring home one of those cute mom interview sheets.

You know the ones. They make you realize all the yelling and moments when you've felt like the worst version of your mom self, do not truly make an impression on your kids. They tune all of that out, for the most part.

They remember that you like coffee or, to your embarrassment, inform their teachers that you really enjoy wine. They think in your spare time you like to fold laundry, and they guess that you're 16 years old. They also firmly believe you're the most beautiful mama on the planet, who likes to do things to make them happy. Pull out those answer sheets anytime you begin to feel mom guilt or a sense of failure.

In your children's eyes, you are amazing.

Remember that.

When my oldest was two, his preschool teacher had each student create a handprint out of paint. Next to it read, "This is the hand you used to hold when I was only two years old."

That little purple painted hand, strung on a piece of matching yarn, stayed propped up on my hutch for years. Each time I passed by, it gave me pause, reminding me how slowly and quickly time simultaneously passed.

And as I sit here writing this book about these baby and toddler chapters of my life, right before my eyes my boys are growing up yet again. They have no more time for "baby shows" like *Mickey Mouse Clubhouse* and would rather climb trees and play soccer than tinker with most of their toys. We are moving into the next phase of parenthood, which will bring a new set of joys, challenges, chaos, and love. Taming the temper tantrums will be replaced with teaching them how to manage friendships and include others on the playground.

We no longer have naps, diapers, sippy cups, footed pajamas, or five-point harness car seats. We have traded in the three-seat stroller for a wagon that hauls our camping chairs and cooler for an afternoon of back-to-back soccer games.

In many ways it's taken forever to get here, and yet sometimes it still feels like yesterday that I held that little hand painted in purple. So far, they still want to hold my hand, and these days, when they do, I squeeze onto them, almost attempting to make a muscle memory of my own, of them at six and nine. I stare at their dirty fingernails that they've chewed down to the quick like little monkeys. As I look at them, I realize in a few short years I'll be dropping car keys into those same hands. They will look a lot different by then, with hair on their knuckles and all. Their nails may still be less than manicure-worthy, but this is life with boys. I'm sure I'll analyze them once more then, realizing those same hands will soon carry a diploma, then leave home, venture into the world, and eventually hold someone else's with love.

When that time comes, how will I feel?

While some people fear death, I fear the day my boys leave home. Because when that time finally comes, the loud craziness of my house will fall silent. The idea that one day I'll wake up and have no one to cook for, or no massive to-do list that includes trips to Costco to feed my army, makes my heart hurt. How do I know how I'll feel in the future, when my children are still so young? Because each time I go away for a girls' weekend, I'm so excited to get away I scream it from the rooftop. But 24 hours into the trip, I miss my rascals like crazy.

Motherhood is strange like that.

My husband actually makes fun of me, because anytime we go away for the weekend I turn into a sobbing mess when I see other blond-haired little boys running around with their folks. It makes me miss mine to the core.

The constant on-the-go of running them here and there will cease. And when I look back at this motherhood journey I've been on, will I be happy knowing I did everything I wanted to do with them? Will I feel satisfied that I got in every snuggle, every spontaneous trip for ice cream? I wonder if I'll ask myself, *Did we celebrate everything? Did we soak it all in? Did we love fiercely? Or did we allow stress and society to get in the way of completely being present together?*

Having now learned to laugh and let go of the craziness of motherhood, I think I will look back with pride and fulfillment, knowing I didn't waste a single moment, enjoying my kids at every stage.

The future for us is unknown, but the potential outline is clear. No matter what our story is, we can make this parenting ride the highlight of our lives.

Love your people fiercely. Stop comparing. Stop giving a rip what others are doing or what they think of you. At the end of the day—and, one day, your life—only one thing will matter: the people you love and the quality of the time you spent with them.

ACKNOWLEDGMENTS

I would like to thank my precious boys, John, Tommy, Teddy, and Nate for loving me so deeply and giving me all the material in the world to write this book. I will keep copies for your one-day wives so they can see what kind of ridiculousness they're in for. I'd like to thank my wonderful husband, Mark, for supporting me throughout this experience and life. A huge thanks goes out to Kelley Kitley for not only helping me face my own anxieties through therapy, but also for supporting me through this process and writing the amazing forward. My mom, Pam Tognetti, has provided endless support and reassurance—throughout this book-writing process and life in general. Thank you, Mom, for always answering my 10,000 phone calls daily and being there for me. I couldn't do this without you. To my mother-in-law, Jean Cuthbert, thank you for your constant support, one-liners, and laughs. You're a huge part of my life and I appreciate all of your wisdom throughout the years. Thank you to my siblings Juliette and Jay for always making me laugh, and to my dad, John Tognetti, for providing me with a Swiss-Italian temper and sense of humor. Thank you nanny-extraordinaire, Kari Kirilova. Without your love and help I'm not sure we would have survived the early years, and I love seeing you now beam with pride as a mother of your own. We love you.

To all my mom tribes in Hinsdale, San Antonio, California, and around the country, thank you for helping me laugh through the motherhood journey. If anyone ever challenges the authenticity of the stories in this book, I'll send them to you all since you know first-hand the times these shenanigans have gone down. A huge thank you to my fellow writers/friends who have supported me on this journey, including Eva Moore, Candice Curry, and the amazing team at Alamo City Moms. You are the purest example of what it means for women to support women, and I am forever grateful. Thank you to Jessica Mewborne for always capturing my family at its best, Taylor Henderson for meticulously editing this book, and Melissa Brown of Sour Pea Design for our amazing cover.

ABOUT THE AUTHOR

Christie Cuthbert has a journalism degree from California State University, Chico, and has been a writer for 16 years. She has written for numerous publications throughout the United States, including *the Gilroy Dispatch, Kentucky New Era, Hollister Freelance, The Hinsdalean Newspaper, Chicago Parent, Harvard Business School's Harbus, Scary Mommy, Today Show Parenting Team, San Antonio Woman Magazine, 78209 Magazine*, and *Alamo City Moms.* She was a 2019 cast member of the stage performance, *Listen to Your Mother,* and has appeared on multiple podcasts including Reality Life with Kate Casey and Woven. She resides in San Antonio with her husband and four boys. You can find more about her on www.christiecuthbert.com

facebook.com/momifartedinchurch

instagram.com/christiecuthbert